EMERGING

A memoir

Alison Rogan

Maelynn
Havelin

ISBN: 979-8-9892440-0-3
ISBN: 979-8-9892440-1-0
ISBN: 979-8-9892440-2-7

Front cover image by Sarah Sanscrainte

Printed by Amazon Kindle Direct, Inc.

First printing edition 2024.

www.emerginglayla.com

This book is dedicated to the ones sitting bedside. Remember, hope is stronger than fear.

A LETTER FROM LAYLA

I used to think I was invincible.

I used to think nothing could take me down.

Turns out, I was wrong.

I don't remember anything from the day of my accident, but that's probably a good thing. I've seen all the pictures and heard everyone's accounts. Still, it feels like I'm looking at someone else's story.

From my perspective, I woke up one day, and everything was different. I had a whole new set of limitations I didn't have before, and honestly, I'd never liked limitations. All of a sudden, I had to count on other people for everything, including reminding me who I was before all this started.

In many ways, it made me a different person. There are parts of the old me I chose not to keep and some I was forced to let go of against my will. I'm still me, but I'm learning who that is every day.

Your perspective really changes after going through something like I did.

I wish I could tell you how it all happened, but I was asleep for most of it.

I know one thing, though:

God was by our side the entire time.

INTRODUCTION

Two things I swore I'd never do: get married or have children.

The thought of having children terrified me; the thought of failing them even more. Marriage and parenting weren't exactly modeled well for me growing up. I knew that I never wanted a child to feel the way I did in my own childhood. I never considered things like illnesses, traumas, or tragedies that could happen with kids. No, I only worried about emotional pain. I only worried that *I* wouldn't be enough for them—that *I* would leave them with scars like my own. I convinced myself I was unfit to ever be a mother, and that was that.

I should've known better, huh?
Never say never, right?

I ended up getting married to a boy I met at a concert, Jeremiah. He was a free spirit, and I was a planner. He brought out a side in me I didn't realize was there. He was old fashioned in comparison to guys I typically dated. He opened doors for me and snuck gas money into my purse. Of course, I had prided myself on my independence back then. I had a goal and a plan, and it didn't involve anyone taking care of me. But when he did it? Well, it just felt right.

I also ended up having those kids I swore I wouldn't—three of them! Motherhood was not something I took lightly. I wanted to be the best version of myself for these three little people. We became parents very young—too young according to most people—and I wanted to prove to everyone we could do it. All parenting styles differ, but I think most can agree we all want to give our children a life better than we had. That was my motivation at least. I was determined to check every box and read every parenting book to figure this parenting thing out. I wanted my kids to have every single thing I was missing as a child. I wanted to be the best version of myself for them. I was going to master this somehow.

Looking back, I was naïve to think that it works like that. Being a parent comes with lots of things you cannot possibly prepare for and emotions so intense there are not words that exist for them. There is no how-to book or instruction manual to actually help you here. Because parenting (and life!) will throw a lot of curve balls at you.

Our daughter, Layla, was born October 13th, 2006 (which also happened to be my birthday). She is the middle child of our group and my first girl. To be honest, we were nervous about having a girl. I am by no means a girly girl. You won't find anything pink in my closet, and I'm worse than a toddler about wearing a dress. Her brother was almost five by that point, and we had grown accustomed to being boy parents. Jeremiah always said we'd have all boys (as if we had any control over that!). A girl was not part of our plan. I mean, how was I supposed to raise a girl?

Looking back, I laugh at us. From the day she was born, she owned anyone who held her, especially her dad. She had these piercing blue eyes and a perfectly proportioned face, almost like a doll. She was impossible not to fall in love with. Just like that, I no longer cared about the pink being everywhere. I'd sworn this girl wouldn't be girly, but she gave me no choice. She changed the whole temperature in our home, and I loved it.

From the day she could figure out words, that child wanted to be heard. She was impossible to ignore, and quickly, we learned what an excellent negotiator she was. She covered our home in anything that sparkled; there could never be enough dresses and shoes for her. She lived in a constant state of motion, always dancing and singing. She questioned everyone, everything, everywhere. There was nothing she believed she couldn't do, and typically, she was right. She dominated most things she tried, and she picked up everything so quickly. We were

4

constantly signing her up for activities, hoping to harness some of that energy and figure out what she liked. The problem? She seemed to like it all!

By the age of nine, that girl did everything from the chess team to surfing, but the activity she seemed most drawn to was cheerleading. She loved the tumbling and performing. She loved being in front of a crowd, and she played into the audience like a seasoned professional. The kid obviously had a gift, so we nurtured it. On average, we spent 4-5 days a week in the gym. She would sign up for every extra class or lesson she could and still beg for more. I would sit in the stands to watch her practices. That girl would fall on her face 50 times in a row and keep getting back up until she perfected a skill. She was the first one to arrive and the last one to leave (and usually, the gym had to turn the lights off to make that happen). Many times, we thought she would burn out, but she never did. For Layla, every moment had to be filled with some kind of activity and some way to keep her moving.

It was a lot to keep up with.

Of course, this energy extended outside the gym, too. Layla excelled in school as well. It came easy to her, and thankfully, very early on her teachers recognized her gifts. Like in everything else, she would only accept perfection when it came to her grades. She would argue her way from a 99 to a 100 on an assignment every single time. Both were still an A, but that 1% meant a lot to her. That 1% represented imperfection. And to Layla, that wasn't acceptable. If she wasn't the best, she'd outwork everybody around her to get there. There was nothing we could say to talk her out of it.

She was truly fearless.

If I'm being honest, having a kid like that is intimidating. Her dad and I are pretty low maintenance, and we are content camouflaging into a room. But having Layla often put the spotlight on us. We were now known as, "Layla's parents." Though we were proud, it wasn't always easy. Layla was bold and intense, and sometimes her peers didn't respond well to how up front she was. I used to tell her she wouldn't be everyone's cup of tea, but she couldn't take the idea of someone not liking her. She wanted it all—the friends, the perfectionism, the achievements, the big, amazing life. Throughout my life I've volunteered with kids of all ages, but I had never seen anyone like my own daughter. Often, I got the same feedback from teachers and parents about her. I read everything I could on raising a strong-willed child, but with each piece of information or advice I'd take in, I'd think, *they don't know my Layla.*

I knew she was special.
I knew she was destined for something great in her future.
If we could just help her manage the intensity, we could guide her safely forward.

As it turned out, that would be much easier said than done.

By the time Layla was finishing her freshmen year in May of 2022, life was settling for our family. Our oldest, also Jeremiah, had just moved out and taken a job as a firefighter in north Florida. Cali, our sweet, empathetic, sporty youngest, was finishing her 4th grade year.
As expected, Layla blended into the high school setting with ease. She had become even more confident in who she was and stood firm on her beliefs, even when these beliefs weren't the popular ones. She was excelling with her grades. She was on the varsity cheer team. She was frequently busy with her friends and always seemed to have plans.

We were proud of the little humans we were raising. There was a lot of trial and error, but no irreparable casualties in our parenting. They were each so different, but all so confident in who they were. Not a bad turnout for two kids who were entirely too young to become parents, huh?

We felt like we were winning at the parent game.

It's dangerous being too confident when it comes to parenting. You don't want to be overprotective, and you don't want to totally let go. You have to walk a fine line between the two. I always wanted my kids to live their life to the fullest and experience it all (within reason of course).

Unfortunately, you can't control everything. You have to send them out into the world and pray for the best.

So, that's what we did.

Only that day, I had no idea that it would be the last time we would see the Layla we knew.

That's the thing about tragedies…

You never know they're coming.

THE ACCIDENT

Day 1: Sunday, May 22nd

We were having a family beach day.

Or at least we were supposed to be.

Cali, Jeremiah, and myself had made our way down to the beach that day (a benefit of being a Florida resident). We'd planned for Layla to join us, but she'd spent the night with friends and made it very clear she wasn't ready to come home. The ride to the beach was spent with her promising me on the phone she'd get a ride there later. Of course, I was disappointed, but I didn't want to start the day getting into an argument with her. She was at that stage of teenager where arguments were a daily thing. On this day, I didn't have the energy to have one, so I gave in. I agreed to let her spend the morning with friends and meet us later. She'd still get there eventually, and I would get the family beach day I wanted.

Looking back now, I wish I'd chosen the argument.
I wish I'd made her come.

When the rest of us got to the beach, we found a parking spot right on the boardwalk. It's one of those spots that's never available—the ones I always wondered how early you had to arrive to get them. I remember thinking, *This is our lucky day.*

Yeah… right.

As soon as we found a piece of real estate in the sand for relaxing, Layla was texting asking to be picked up. This was typical teenage stuff; her plans changed by the moment and at everyone's expense. For whatever reason, her ride had fallen through, and now, she was ready to come home. But we were 40 minutes away from her, and Cali and I were just getting ready to go hunting for beach glass. So, I told Layla she would need to wait. Then, I braced myself for her reply. Honestly, I had to laugh at the persistence of this girl. I knew she was not going to give up until I gave her a concrete plan, so ultimately, I asked her to give us an hour, and reluctantly, she agreed to wait.

That settled, I went back to sea glass hunting with Cali. Only a few minutes into our hunt, I heard my phone making a strange sound. When I made my way back to grab it, someone was trying to call me from Facebook. I was unaware that was even possible! When I told Jeremiah, he told me it was probably an accidental call and encouraged me to put my phone away so I could give Cali all my attention.

I don't know how I knew it, but I swear to you I did.
Something was wrong.

I immediately called Layla, but I got no answer. I texted her, but I got no reply. Because I had talked to her only 15 minutes before, her silence was alarming. So, I opened my phone's tracking app to see where she could be, praying it was somewhere that would have clearly caused her to miss my call.

Because she never missed my calls.

I saw then that she wasn't at her friend's house, but she was close by, still in the neighborhood. Conveniently, I knew someone who lived right near where she was, so I sent my friend, David, a text.

Me: Can you peek out the front door and tell my daughter to answer her phone?

12

My phone rang instantly in reply.

My heart was officially in my throat as I answered David's call. He immediately tried to calm me, telling me not to worry. He said there was an ATV accident that had just happened down the street, and a crowd had gathered. He kept assuring me that Layla must be there watching it unfold.

Again, I don't know how I knew it, but I swear to you I did.
It was her.

I asked David to do the impossible: to walk down to the accident and confirm where my daughter was in all of this. To his horror—to all of our horror—what he found as he approached the wreckage was that Layla was involved. She was hurt very badly.

"They're taking her to St. Mary's hospital, and they're going by trauma hawk," he told me shakily. "Ali, you need to hurry."

I will never forget Jeremiah's face as he started packing up our stuff as quickly as possible, trying not to break down in the process. I was doing plenty of that for both of us. Cali was silent, robotic almost. She was trying to put the pieces together with us. I was dialing numbers frantically, trying to get more information. We had little details about what happened or how it happened, but we knew enough to know the girls involved were badly injured. They wouldn't be airlifted if things were going to be okay.

We were jolted out of shock on our drive to the hospital when my phone rang again. This time, it was her friend's mother calling to tell me what I already knew: It was in fact our Layla, and she was not okay.

"It's bad," she cried over and over again.

It's bad. That's what was running through my mind on repeat when we finally pulled into the hospital. There we saw the trauma hawk landing right as we wheeled into a parking spot.

13

"That's her," Jeremiah whispered as he watched the chopper settle.

I looked back at Cali. She seemed so young, so afraid in that moment. I wondered how we were going to manage whatever we found beyond those hospital doors. This would break her; it might break all of us. I grabbed her little hands and prayed. Then, I did what I think any parent might do in that moment: I lied. I told my little girl that everything was going to be fine. Why? Because I knew Cali was not equipped to handle this.

She needed her mom, but so did Layla. So, I gave Cali the next best thing. I called my best friend Jenna and asked her to come get my youngest girl while we figured out what would happen with my oldest waiting inside.

Jeremiah waited with Cali for Jenna to come while I ran toward the helicopter, where I was quickly stopped and redirected to the emergency room doors. Foolishly I thought explaining I was her mother would grant me some special access. The paramedics didn't care that I wanted to hug and kiss my girl; they were trying to save her life and get her moved inside to the trauma team.

So, I finally gave up and went inside the emergency room. I could hardly find the right words to explain why I was there when asked. I expected to be rushed immediately to her side, but instead, I was directed to go sit in the waiting room with everyone else. This seemed impossible to me. There was no way I could wait any longer, and I told every single person who worked in the ER that very thing. My pleas fell on deaf ears. With nothing to do but wait, I sat down in defeat alone with my thoughts.

I sat as close as I could to those doors leading to the patients. I knew Layla was somewhere behind them, so I waited with my eyes glued to them. I watched doctors come out and summon people over and over, but my name wasn't called. I started to imagine charging the doors the next time someone swiped their badge and opened it. I figured if I ran fast enough, I could get to her before security got to me. The idea was getting more and more tempting as I grew more and more desperate.

Finally, it happened. A woman with a kind face came through those doors and headed directly toward me.

"Ali, my name is Kathleen," she said warmly. "Let's go find your baby."

In that moment, it was like she'd been sent from God Himself. She was the sister of my neighbor who my friend Jenna had alerted of our situation. Kathleen was the assistant nurse manager of ICU stepdown. She watched Layla being lowered in the trauma hawk and came right down. Now, she was here to help.

On shaky legs, I stood and followed Kathleen through those doors and into the trauma wing of the hospital. She sat me in what looked like a nurse's office, got me some water, and told me to wait for her while she went to find my Layla. Again, I was waiting, but at least now I was closer to my girl. There were no more locked doors, no more strangers surrounding me, no more uncertainty as to who would help me. Kathleen's presence and effort made me feel better, so much so that when she came back, I broke down completely.

"Is my daughter going to die?" I cried repeatedly.

I was rambling about all these personal things to this stranger turned comforter as if I was in a therapy session. Likely unsure what else to do, Kathleen sat down and wrapped me up in the biggest hug. I'm not usually a hugger, especially with a stranger, but I think she knew I needed that hug more than I did.

As Jeremiah finally arrived inside, I was excited to introduce him to our new ally. Kathleen briefed us on where we were going before leading us down the hall to one of the trauma bays. These rooms don't look like normal hospital rooms. You can almost sense the amount of tragedy those walls have seen as you pass by them. There are equipment and machines everywhere, so the hospital can be prepared for any situation that comes through those doors. There were large, red tool chests against the walls that seemed out of place to me. It looked like something you'd find in a garage, and I wondered what kind of things were kept inside. Could they rebuild a person with tools like a carpenter? It was all surreal, almost like what you'd expect to see on one of those medical TV shows.

Only this was real life. *My* life.

As we stepped inside a room, I was surprised at the quiet we found waiting for us. My eyes followed the bright light to the middle of the room where, in the center of that space, was my daughter.

The first thing I noticed was the neck brace. It was so large compared to her tiny frame and it appeared to be covering her mouth. There was a tube running out of the neck brace connected to bigger tubes plugged into bigger machines, which I later learned was because she was intubated. She had blood spatter all over her face and hair. Her eyes were closed as if she was only sleeping. She was covered with a white blanket, but her tiny, bruised hands were exposed enough to reveal a hospital bracelet that read, "Juliet Trauma." They didn't know her name when she arrived, so they gave her this one. Tubes and wires seemed to be coming out every inch of her. Lying there still and quiet, she looked so fragile, so much so that I had to squelch every urge to crawl in the bed and squeeze her tight. Kathleen tried explaining what was happening to me, but nothing she said made sense. This whole situation didn't make sense. My mind couldn't process what I was seeing. Our Layla was strong— the strongest girl I knew—and this girl in front of me looked beaten and barely alive.

There was a lot of empty space around her bed except for a single chair on either side of her. I wondered who put them here, as they didn't seem to belong in the room. I imagine someone did it for us before we entered, which felt like the sweetest gesture at the time. I sat in the chair next to her bedside, touching her as gently as possible, searching her face for a sign she was in there, and promising her we were there and that everything would be okay. At my words, one tear fell from her right eye. They told me it was a reflex, but I didn't believe that. I still don't. I knew then and I know now: Our girl heard us that day before she slipped further into a coma.

On the drive to the hospital, I had called Layla's boyfriend's mom, Amanda. She was a paramedic, and I was desperate for resources. It was the first time I had ever reached out to her since the kids had been dating. I selfishly didn't think of how her son was going to handle this news or the burden I had just put on this woman. I just needed answers or, at the very least, someone with experience that could help me. I started to panic when I felt my phone vibrate and saw her name on the screen.

"We're in the waiting room…"

What had I done? Did I just drag someone else into our nightmare? Was I really that selfish? In my head, I justified it because I needed help. She offered to come, and I wanted every resource I could find. It was evident my daughter needed a lot of help.

I had only met Amanda once before, but I knew their family was kind to my daughter, and, according to Layla, they were my kind of people. She had been pushing the idea of Amanda and I becoming friends for a while, so it seemed ironic that she was the one who finally brought us together after all, even under these circumstances. I collected Amanda and her son in the waiting room and walked them to Layla, braced for their reactions. I figured I was going to have to get used to people's reaction to the sight of her if anyone was going to see her like this.

Their response was not what I expected.

Amanda was calm and collected. She knew the appropriate questions to ask the doctors and repeatedly told us that Layla was going to live. She refused to believe anything but total restoration, and she prayed over Layla with such conviction that I almost believed her. It was a Sunday, and as the prayers went up, I remember thinking, *Layla will be home by Friday.* In my naivete then, I couldn't imagine this lasting longer than a week. I think you almost have to slip into a level of insanity to get through this reality.

17

The doctors were describing so much about our girl's condition that sounded like nonsense.

Brain bleeds…
Carotid artery…
Broken jaw…
Internal bleeding…

Finally, they told us what would happen next.

"She's got to move upstairs into ICU," one said.

So, we followed behind her like a funeral procession.

For the first time, I noticed two men in regular clothes walking close behind me. They addressed us by name and introduced themselves as the detectives on this case. That's when I saw the brown bag one was holding. I knew this bag; I've seen it before. Not this exact one, but one just like it. Years ago, I lost my little brother tragically and a detective handed me the same brown lunch bag containing his belongings then. That day I felt like I was there all over again, and it made me sick. I took the bag with shaking hands and opened it. Inside were Layla's shoes and the stack of the signature bracelets she always wore that had been cut off her arms. My first thought was how upset she was going to be that they ruined her collection. Each bracelet had been gifted or handpicked by her over the years, and now they were just a pile of colorful strings.

Nothing was the same anymore.

I was still covered in sunscreen and sand but had no intention of leaving my girl's side. So, after Jeremiah got me settled in the room, he headed home to get me clean clothes. By now, the staff had cleaned Layla up a little. The blood spatter was wiped from her face and only little cuts were visible now. They had removed the neck brace, so I could clearly see the tube in her mouth. It was attached to her face with fasteners stuck to her cheeks, keeping her lungs filled with air. There were still wires coming out of her everywhere, but now there was a stack of grey boxes attached to a pole on her right side all administrating different medications labeled with words I had never seen before. They had little lights and numbers all over them like some kind of morbid Christmas tree. To her left was another machine making a noise we will never forget: It was the ventilator. On the screens were green lines representing the breaths it gave her—the breaths it breathed for her.

In that moment, an unexpected thought came into my head.

Remember how scared you were to have children?

That young, naïve version of me was so afraid I wouldn't measure up as a mom. So scared of the harm and damage I might do to my kids. Those fears now seemed like nothing to me. I never imagined motherhood would include this. This was something so horrific that I'm not sure my brain could've conjured it up.

Then, another thought followed just as quickly.

If I knew then that this was going to happen now, would I still have chosen this? Would I still have become a mom?

Without hesitation, I whispered, "Yes."

I loved being my kids' mom more than anything I have ever done. I loved every day of the 15 years I was given with Layla up to that point. Even in this pain, I wouldn't want to give that back. I just couldn't picture a world where she didn't exist as my girl.

My thoughts were interrupted with the arrival of her doctor. Honestly, I was very confused about her diagnosis at that point. In my head, she made it upstairs, so something must be going right. I'm usually pretty good at seeing the silver lining. This first doctor, however, wanted me to know clearly that the silver lining wasn't yet in sight. He was relentless in making me understand how serious this was. He was direct about the likely ending we'd meet. I was advised to notify my family and make our peace with it. After dropping that emotional grenade, he quietly left the room. In that moment, I was defeated. I was hopeless. I couldn't breathe.

I called Jeremiah, trying to reiterate what the doctor had told me, but all I could really say was, "They said she's going to die."

I knew I needed to update the rest of our family, but I couldn't pick up the phone. I didn't want to say those words out loud. Somehow texting felt safer. Everyone asks what they can do for you in these scenarios. I think it's because they feel as helpless as the person on the other end of the phone. So, every time they asked, I just answered the only way I knew how: prayers. I myself fell to my knees at her bedside to do just that. This wasn't really praying; it was more like begging. I would have mortgaged anything for her life in that moment. I offered my own life, willing to make any deal with God if I could just keep her alive.

I didn't really grow up with a relationship with God. That came later in my life. I wasn't even sure I was asking right or if my prayers were good enough for Him to hear me. I did know one thing though: The doctors were unable to fix this. They admittedly couldn't give me what I wanted. So, I was going to have to take this higher. I needed a miracle. I figured if I could get enough voices praying for her then God had to hear it. In the back of my mind, I had doubts though. I wondered what made me think I deserved a miracle. I hadn't dedicated my life to service or anything like that. I could hardly quote the Bible, and I'm too shy to pray in front of people. I am an ordinary person. Before that day, statistically speaking, I didn't think any more traumas could come to my life. Yet here we were. So, doubt and all, I had nowhere else to turn but above.

By the time Jeremiah returned with some clean clothes, the neurosurgeon arrived to brief us. We could quickly tell this doctor specialized in her injury. He was not as aggressive as the last one, but he still made it clear that this was serious. He explained the next 72 hours would be critical. 72 hours didn't seem like enough time to make our peace. We would be watching for seizures, brain swelling, and neurostorming. These were all things able to take her life and likely to happen given the severity of her injuries. She also had broken her jaw and damaged her right carotid artery. There were multiple brain bleeds. There was liver damage and internal bleeding to deal with, too. She needed blood transfusions as well. It felt like the list kept growing. It was like a race toward what would kill her first.

We've all seen movies like this, haven't we? The ones with people in a coma who sleep peacefully before waking up confused but refreshed. The ones with happy endings. This didn't look like that. This was much worse; it was real life. They leave this part out in the movies.

The surgeon went on to specifically prepare us for Layla's first surgery that night. A bolt would be placed in her head to monitor cranial pressure. If her brain swelled, then an additional surgery would follow to open her skull and relieve the pressure. Seems like a silly thing to worry about at that time, but all I could think about was the fact that they'd have to shave her head. Her beautiful hair that she loved so much would be gone. For some reason, that detail was almost too much to bear.

They asked me and Jeremiah to step out while they got to work. There isn't a waiting room in ICU. Other than her room, there's nowhere to sit, and you need to be buzzed in each time you leave the unit. We wandered out of the unit into the hall and found a little bench someone had donated for anxious waiting parents like us, I imagined. Throughout the course of this, that bench would become our makeshift time out spot. The place we'd go to take a break, share our fears, cry on each other's shoulders. That day, I was rattling off all my fears while Jeremiah mostly sat in silence. It was all we knew to do.

When we were finally allowed back in, I could see the missing patch of hair on Layla's right side. This is where the monitor was drilled into her skull. It stuck up out of her head like an antenna and had a wire running from it plugged in somewhere like a cell phone charger. Along with it came another grey box with another screen we had to watch and more beeps to add to the sounds in the room. We were watching for cranial pressure and hoping the number didn't climb high enough to require surgery. Jeremiah was a lot better with the machines than I was. He picked it up with ease while all I saw was chaos. I couldn't escape the noises though. No one forgets those sounds. I think that's because everything in the room seemed to be making noises except the one thing we needed to hear from: our daughter. She just lay there completely still and silent while the machines kept her alive.

Eventually Jeremiah kissed us goodbye to collect Cali and head home, and I settled into the first night of our journey. The ICU had this little chair that reclined into a bed (not that anyone does much sleeping there). As I prepared it for myself for the night, I cried. Honestly, I broke down any time someone entered the room. Most nurses were kind enough to sit and comfort me. In any other situation, I would hate sympathy from strangers, but here, I craved it. I was desperate for it even. I wanted someone to tell me something positive. I wanted to hear someone say there was a possibility. The best I got that night was from a kind ICU nurse.

"We see miracles all the time."

I looked up the definition of the word "miracle" and felt even more hopeless: "a highly improbable event." I can't even describe the emptiness and desperation I felt at the wording. "Highly impossible" wasn't what I wanted to hear.

Now, sleep was definitely out of the question. That night, I sat up next to Layla and talked. I pleaded with her to find her way back to us. I prayed like I have never prayed before, begging God to keep her heart beating. I told her how much we loved her, hoping she could hear me.

Other than a few interactions with nurses, it was just me and the sounds in that room. Occasionally I'd hear the trauma hawk bringing someone else in, reminding me of how this day started. Someone else was beginning their own nightmare. What a terrible place this was. I always thought of hospitals as places babies were born, not places you lose them. I guess it's a matter of perspective; now, I was getting a strong dose of reality.

Agonizingly, I watched night turn into day. As the sun came up, I finally exhaled.

She made it through the night.
It was a step in the right direction, and I needed something to celebrate.

THE ICU

Day 2: Monday, May 23rd

Jeremiah was back the next morning, but it was almost like we didn't recognize each other. We both were running on no sleep and neither of us was processing this very well. We didn't have the energy or the words to comfort each other, so we mostly sat in silence. I'm sure his emptiness mirrored mine. We both felt like we failed her. We couldn't protect our little girl, and now, it was like we were being punished for that. It's hard to imagine the rest of the world was still turning beyond the ICU walls when it felt like ours had stopped. There was a revolving door of parents doing the same thing we were on that ICU floor while the rest of the world walked around oblivious. This was a side of life I had never thought about. A place I had never imagined.

Children should outlive their parents.

Later that morning Jenna arrived (which of course she did). She's the friend I call on for *everything*. We've lived on the same street for 20 years, and Layla and my kids are like family to her. I didn't ask her to come; I was feeling a lot of guilt about asking. I didn't want to put those images in anyone else's head. Why should they suffer what I'm suffering? Thankfully, Jenna knows me better than most so she knew I wouldn't ask. She typically respects my no hugging rule, too, but this day was different. I met her outside the ICU doors actively looking forward to that hug.

"I got you," she whispered in my ear, and I knew she meant it.

This wouldn't be the first time Jenna had to put me back together. She'd been by my side for other tragedies along the way, just like a best friend would be. As I led her into the room, I watched her reaction to seeing Layla, someone she loved so much. Jenna tried to keep her usual composed self, but it was useless. So, she had her first cry, letting it all out, before she got down to the business of being a best friend.

Over the course of Layla's time in the ICU, Jenna was there. She helped us decipher and remember what doctors were saying. She knew the right questions to ask. She tried to get us to eat and drink. She brought me priests, and pastors, and therapy dogs. She responded to my texts and kept updates going out to others. She even filled my role of room mom in Cali's classroom. I'm older than Jenna by a few years, but Cali always thought I was younger because she said Jenna was more mature than me. This is true. I was afraid of my own shadow, but Jenna was brave, really brave. She was always pushing me outside my comfort zone and teaching me not to live in fear. This was no different. I often wished I could be more like her but having her as a friend was an acceptable compromise. She was the perfect person for this moment in our lives.

That day, the ICP monitor was still reading stable. Layla's brain wasn't swelling, and she wasn't having any more seizures. You'd think that would be something to celebrate, but doctors seemed confused by it. Turns out, this is not what typically happens, especially with an injury this severe, so they were puzzled. It felt like no activity was worse than bad activity. No activity was strange in this case. They knew how to manage seizures and brain swelling, but our girl was doing nothing.

Nothing until the neurostorming started.

Neurostorming happens when your nervous system has difficulties regulating after a brain injury. In Layla's case, her temperature started spiking, her blood pressure was all over the place, and her heartbeat would not regulate. The machines were extra noisy, and another grey box was added to her Christmas tree of medications. It felt like nurses were constantly rushing in to address the alarms going off while we just sat there helpless. Her temperature climbed too high, so they had to lay her on a cooling blanket with bags of ice piled on her little body. Her skin was cold and rock hard, reminding me of the fish we kept on ice after our many fishing trips in the Keys.

She didn't feel alive.

The temperature would come down, so we could remove the ice, but it never lasted long. It would quickly spike again, and we'd start the whole thing over. This became a routine for weeks. The doctors made rounds often. They would check her pupils and reaction to pain. We would brace ourselves each time, hoping she'd do something they wanted, but it wasn't happening. The worst part was the disappointment on everyone's faces each time she failed one of their tests.

Layla was young and had her whole life ahead of her.
It seemed like such a waste to all of us for it to be cut so short.

Day 3: Tuesday, May 24th

Amanda had created a Facebook page to help get updates out to friends, family, and internet strangers alike. The news had spread, and our phones were now going crazy. Someone had returned Layla's phone to me. While I didn't have the password to get in, I could see a preview of the messages that constantly came in. Everyone was looking for her to respond in the hopes that it wasn't as bad as the rumors going around made it seem. Everyone wanted some sort of hope, but we had none to give.

She was still alive, so she was still fighting.
That was all we had at that point.

She started taking a few breaths over the ventilator, but the doctors didn't seem as impressed as we were about this. Her breaths would show up as red lines on the machine versus the green ones that represented the ventilator. We would watch that screen waiting for those red lines to appear. Every so often when they did, we would cry. To us, it represented life. Those little red lines literally breathed a little bit of hope back into all of us.

That night there was a prayer vigil scheduled outside her window. I'm not sure I had ever been to one before that, so I wasn't sure what to expect. At the least, Jenna encouraged me to finally wash the sunscreen off my body and make an appearance. Ultimately, I wasn't ready to leave Layla's side. One of our nurses had a solution. She took us to a room on the ICU floor with a bed and a shower for situations like ours. It looked like a tiny hotel room just down the hall from her. Quickly, I showered, anxious to get back to my girl.

When I got back to Layla's room and looked out her window, I was thankful I showered. Down below people were gathering, and I mean a *lot* of people. I was speechless. All these people had come together to pray for our little girl. I knew Layla would have loved this. She would've loved to know what a big deal she was, so much so that I wished she could see it. Layla always loved an audience.

I decided to go down and join them while Jeremiah stayed with Layla. I started to feel hopeful as I made my way down to the parking lot. God had to hear us, right? There were so many people, so many kind words, so many tears. Our little girl meant this much to all these people and knowing that made me feel less alone. Once there, I was passed from one person to another, some I knew and some strangers. A man named Rob introduced himself and asked if I'd like him to get it started. I had no idea what that entailed, but I accepted the offer. Quickly I realized this guy had a gift; he knew his Bible. I thought his words would get God's attention, but instead, they got mine. He led the group in prayer and, even though I was emotional, I started to feel peace.

I changed my prayers that day.

I stopped begging God to spare her. Instead, I prayed that we would just be okay no matter how this ended. I asked God not to leave me. I told Him this was too big, and I needed help. I confessed that I was really scared this would break me. I needed to know he would keep my family together in the aftermath of this. Last, I promised that, no matter how it turned out, I would honor Him and help others going through hardship like this for as long as I lived. And I meant it all, every single world.

Afterwards I went back upstairs to tell Jeremiah all about the prayer vigil. As I spoke, I was excited in a way. I had this vision we were storming heaven's gates for Layla. I felt comfort that we were not alone in this, even if we lost her. Jeremiah had been watching from the window. He even made a sign that read, *"Layla loves you,"* posted up for her supporters below. That vigil recharged us weary parents more than we even realized.

31

Reluctantly after that, I kissed Layla goodnight and headed to my next obstacle. Jeremiah would take over Layla's watch. It was time to go home to Cali and give her some answers.

Watching Cali suffer through this was one of the hardest parts. She was too young to handle what was happening but old enough to know something was very wrong. Cali has always been a Momma's girl; talking about her emotions was definitely something she reserved for me. This time, however, I had been gone for days. While Jenna was trying to substitute in my absence, she was running out of board games and distractions to keep Cali calm. The last time I had seen her was when I made my emotional exit from the car in the hospital parking lot. I knew she needed answers, I knew she was in pain, and I knew this wasn't going to be easy.

When I got home, Cali ordered dinner. We had never used a food delivery service before this, but she really was getting accustomed to having her favorite meals at her fingertips with the touch of a button. She ordered this giant pretzel with cheese dip, something I would not have allowed for dinner typically, but all bets were off now. As we got ready for bed, I told her to ask me anything. I never like to lie to my kids, so I try to tell them the truth for the most part, even if the truth is heavy and hard.

This truth was awful though. And Cali hated it as much as I did. She pleaded with me like I pleaded with God. She begged to take Layla's place. She begged for our old life back. It was more painful than I imagined. I couldn't promise Cali anything she wanted. I couldn't grant her relief. I could only promise that we would be okay, even if I wasn't sure what that looked like. I told her that's what I asked God for, and because I don't lie to her, she accepted that as fact.

Still, I knew without a doubt that getting Cali through this was going to take a lot more tears and a lot more Door Dash.

Day 4: Wednesday, May 25th

They named the Facebook page "Layla's Journey."

It became a useful outlet for me for a few different reasons. Eventually I started posting the nightly updates, which was therapeutic for me. I kept notes on her throughout the day, and I would put it all together at night. It gave me something to do. Otherwise, I felt so useless just sitting there watching others care for her. The page was growing quite fast, too. Amanda helped manage it and created the hashtags #laylastrong and #brighterdaysarecoming. I loved scrolling through everyone's pictures, comments, and emails with those hashtags. It seemed like something Layla would have loved. The page kept everyone updated in one place, so I didn't have to keep repeating the same conversations.

Layla always teased that Facebook was for old people, so it made me giggle when her friends started joining the page, too. One of the students had come up with the idea: "Wear Pink for Layla Day." Layla loved everything in pink. Throughout the day pictures came rolling in of students in their pink attire. And it wasn't just at Layla's school. The movement had spread through the county at other schools. Cheer gyms were doing it, athletic teams were doing it, adults were sending in pictures. Even her preschool, elementary school, and middle school joined in. Online, there was a sea of pink taking over the page. Every time I visited the site, there were more pictures going up. "Pink for Layla" was spreading all over. Something about it brought me comfort.

Our cousin created a 24-hour prayer chain. Anyone had the option of signing up for one of the 20-minute time slots. For 24 hours straight (and I mean throughout the night, too), there would be prayers going up for Layla. "Layla Strong" t-shirts were even being sold. Always made me laugh seeing all the men in those pink shirts. One fundraiser started with pink bows that the community started tying to trees. Driving home night after night we would see the bows leading up to our house. Some kids had even sidewalk chalked all over our driveway and street. Everywhere I turned, we had so much love and support. It was overwhelming in the best way. I just couldn't get my head around it— how all these people showed up for us. Every time I saw another picture, I would think how much Layla would love this and I hoped one day I could show her.

As night fell, we had gotten through another day. She was still not regulating her temperature and the neurostorming was relentless. Still, she was taking more breaths on her own, and we were celebrating every single one of those red lines. Settling in to try and sleep, I gathered my notes and did my first Facebook post.

I have to be honest. This is emotionally exhausting. Waiting for some sign she's in there. Hoping she will do what the doctors need her to. Patience is not my strong suit. Waiting for her to show us some sign she's coming back. Lots of waiting, lots of ups and downs, lots of moments of debilitating sadness followed by small victories. To our family, friends, community, and new friends we've gained through this, we thank you for the support and helping carry us through. I just can't say thank you enough because it hits me constantly how grateful I am, how many have just come through for us in all sorts of ways, and how much she's going to love knowing what a big deal she is because she wouldn't want to miss this. Sorry, I had to get that out because you all should know that you really are amazing.

Day 5: Thursday, May 26th

Layla never sat quietly.

That's what made it even stranger to see her lying there so still. I finally understood how silence could be so loud. Her absence was everywhere. I missed her voice, I missed looking at her eyes, I even missed the music she played too loud. Her things were still scattered all over the house. Her Starbucks half empty in the fridge, her school bag by the front door, her shoes all over the place. We couldn't even bear to go into her room, so we would just put her things by her door. It felt kind of like what people do on the side of the road after a fatal car crash. I hated the thought her room might end up as a memorial one day. Sure, we clung to hope because she was still with us, but she wasn't showing any signs she'd be coming home. We were constantly on this rollercoaster of highs and lows. We tried to celebrate the little things, but the negative thoughts had ways of creeping in and suffocating you.

Today they would remove the monitor from her head. Her brain still wasn't swelling. I wanted that to be a good thing so bad, but doctors gave us a feeling it might not be. There are so many unknowns with the brain, and hers wasn't responding the way one would in this situation. Then again, she's always done things her way. Once the monitor was out, they could schedule the MRI and find out what kind of damage was in there.

I knew what they feared; we feared it, too.

We stepped out into the hall and headed to our little bench, so they could get to work. I was looking forward to being able to brush Layla's hair. I wanted something that felt normal—some kind of task meant for a mom. Jenna had brought me the supplies I'd need: a hairbrush, dry shampoo, and some strong detangler. I used to tell Layla she washed her hair too much. She would hate being on day five with dirty hair. This felt like something I could finally do to help her.

When we were allowed back in the room, staples had replaced the bolt that was in her head. I guess it was easier to look at than the antenna thing. My son had staples in his head once, the result of hitting his head on the coffee table messing around with friends. We were in and out of the ER within an hour, and he was proud of his battle scar afterward. Maybe one day Layla would be proud of hers, too. I crawled under all the wires to get behind her bed so I could brush her hair. Her blond hair was covered in pink streaks from all the blood she lost in the accident. It was a matted mess of knots, and I was a little overwhelmed at where to start. It's not like I could tell her to pick up her head so I'd have a better angle.

This was going to have to be done methodically.

I started with small sections and combed them out slowly. Handfuls of her hair started coming out into the comb. First, I panicked, wondering if hair loss was a side effect, but I quickly realized this was the section of hair they had shaved and now was matted into the rest of her hair. It took about two hours to get through, but the entire thing made me happy. It was the type of thing I was good at—the type of thing a mother could do.

Jeremiah, on the other hand, was turning into an expert with her medications and machines. Earlier that morning they tested her ability to breathe by shutting off the ventilator briefly and allowing her to take an unassisted breath. It nearly gave Jeremiah a heart attack, but it was also his chance to learn all about that machine. That was the perfect outlet for him. He has always been that type of guy. He can build or fix anything with the help of YouTube. It was difficult for him not to be able to fix her, so learning about what had the potential to fix her was the next best thing. I would listen to him converse with the medical team like they

36

were speaking another language. *He* was speaking their language. It made me smile to see this side of him. I even started calling him Nurse Rogan.

They started lowering her pain medications that morning hoping to see some movement from her. Nurses would come in periodically to do pain tests. They would poke her with things and bend the tips of her fingers, looking to see if she would withdraw from the pain. The Layla we knew would have swatted back at them. It was disheartening each time she wouldn't, but internally, I pacified myself thinking she had a high pain tolerance. She was still intubated, so they also started triggering her gag reflex. Now this, she could do. It was a basic function to them, but I just loved seeing her move.

There was another prayer vigil scheduled that night, this one was started by one of her cheer teams. They put out a call for anyone Layla had ever cheered with to show up. Her cheer teams were always like a sisterhood. She had been cheering from such a young age and at multiple gyms, so it really became her community. I had seen a lot of these girls grow from babies. Now, they would gather and pray for their cheer sister. There were many different gyms being represented with one thing in common: They were here to support one of their own. It was beautiful. Rob once again led the group and gave them an opportunity to pray. Listening to these kids pray really touched me. Their prayers were so innocent and so genuine. Their cries to God were to heal their friend. It was difficult watching kids try to process what happened, but at the same time, it was evident God was with us. Hearts were being changed. Some kids shared with me that this was the first time they had heard anyone talk about God. Others told me they'd never prayed before this, and now, they pray daily. I don't know why this brought me comfort, but it did. I had promised God I'd use this for good, no matter what happened. I guess, in a way, I felt like that promise was being fulfilled in these kids.

If Layla died, it would not be in vain.

By this point there were a ton of people following her story and waiting for the nightly updates. I tried to get them out at a normal hour, but often, I couldn't get to it until after midnight. No matter when I posted, though, I almost instantly got notified people were commenting.

37

No matter what time of day, I wasn't alone. That helped me a lot, which was ironic considering I'd typically hate my business being so public. We had created this online community, and it was becoming something special. It was a place where others shared their own stories and encouraged strangers. Everyone rallied in the hope that we would witness a miracle.

Sometimes, I tried to keep the updates positive. I may have even downplayed how bad it was at times. I figured there was no point in making this sadder; it was already sad. In some ways, keeping the updates positive also kept me positive.

Miss Layla was very busy today. The trauma doctors turned off the ventilator this morning for a brief moment, and our little fighter took a breath on her own. Then the next team of doctors removed the monitor from her head and patched her up. I was able to finally brush her beautiful hair, something she always enjoyed, and I really missed doing. She was doing great breathing today, lots of red lines. This morning, they reduced one of the medications keeping her sedated, and we started to see movements in her shoulders and chest. Quite a few actually, letting them know she didn't want to be bothered. (Just wait till she can talk!) These are small steps but also such victories. She still isn't responding to pain, but it could be the meds. About an hour ago they turned down the pain meds a little more. Hoping to see some more progress soon. She should also be getting her MRI sometime tomorrow which will hopefully give us some answers about the days ahead.

Day 6: Friday, May 27th

When you're in a coma, they put these wrist restraints on you. These are to protect you from waking up and pulling at the many lines or intubation keeping you alive. For some reason, I loved seeing those restraints on Layla. To me, that meant there was still a possibility she was going to wake up. They had weaned her off the majority of the pain medications, and still, she wasn't responding to pain. It was a waiting game. I've never wanted to see her in pain, but in this case, it was her way out of this. She was moving ever so slightly, mostly a gagging movement like she was almost coughing in slow motion. We were constantly encouraging her, kissing her, and letting her know we were there. We took turns hovering over her.

Jeremiah was on her left side kissing her hand when he jumped up with tears in his eyes. She had opened her hand. I immediately began recording so we could show the doctors, but she didn't move it again. It was a small thing, but we were desperate for anything. We needed a few breadcrumbs of hope, and that small open hand felt like just that.

That night, the nurses forgot to put her restraints back on. When we called attention to it, they just gave us a sympathetic look. They no longer feared she was going to wake up and pull at anything.

That was one of the harder days.

Seven years before this, almost to the day, I lost my little brother. It was unexpected, and he was gone before my family was even notified. It was excruciatingly painful. I couldn't imagine ever feeling that low again until this. This was so much worse. My brother's death was quick, while this was like being tortured slowly. It felt cruel in many ways to live in this limbo. I was able to start grieving for my brother immediately, but to grieve Layla felt like giving up.

I ached for relief. Frequently, I cried out to God, "If you're going to take her, just do it already. Why are you torturing us?"

I think having bad days was to be expected. I didn't know it then, but God was working on me, even on those bad days. I had to go through every ounce of this. You know the expression: "God never gives us more than we can handle." Well, that's a lie. Whoever made that up obviously never lost a child. This was a lot bigger than my ability, and I knew it. I had to let go of thinking I was in control of anything and admit I couldn't do this on my own. I had to surrender. I had to lean on my faith and embrace that I couldn't do this without God. Being vulnerable was not something I typically enjoyed, yet being vulnerable kept my sanity.

That night, when I couldn't find the words, my post was brief.

Long night, they slowly weaned her off sedation until about 6:30 this morning. Now it's up to her to wake up. She's still intubated and not responding to pain but also still doing some breaths on her own and moving shoulders and trying to cough. The waiting is brutal honestly. I'm waiting now for them to take her for MRI.

Day 7: Saturday, May 28th

My son had moved almost four hours away in March. He was just 19 at the time and one of the first people I contacted when this happened. We were talking every day, both trying to lift the other one up. It was like maturity had set in overnight for this boy. He always had the kindest words for me. The hospital kept suggesting having Layla's siblings visit in case we lost her, but I was on the fence about it. I didn't think they would be able to handle that, but was it fair of me to take away the opportunity to say goodbye? Did they really need to remember her like this? My son kept bringing it up, asking me if he should come. I know he wanted me to decide for him, but I just couldn't.

When he took the job in another city, we knew the first year he would be on probation. That meant we wouldn't get to see much of him while he proved himself to the department. I hated that this was a bad distraction for him. He was battling a lot of guilt; I think we all were. He and his sister didn't typically get along. Now, he felt like he should have been a better brother. It was heartbreaking to hear him say that. They did fight, but most siblings do, and Layla was not easy to get along with in general. I reminded him of this, but it didn't seem to help. I had almost been steering him away from the idea of coming. I just kept telling him there wasn't much he could do here. Typically, I would jump at any chance to get to see him, but I didn't want this situation to derail the future he was building. So, I told him it had to be his decision. If he felt he needed closure from seeing her, then he should come.

A fireman's schedule is 24 hours on, then 2 days off. I know it sounds appealing, but I learned the downside of that from the account of my son. When you're running calls all night with little sleep, it takes a whole day to recover. The following day you are resetting your sleep schedule, then it all starts over again. Still, he made the decision: His shift was over at 7:00 that morning, and he would be coming straight to the hospital. By this point, the nurses had become our friends, so they'd heard about the son we were so proud of. Now, I was excited to introduce him to our hospital family.

The day before this Layla had finally been taken for her for MRI. We were waiting for the trauma team to arrive and give us some answers as to why she wasn't waking up. By the look on their faces when they finally showed, we knew. There were multiple brain bleeds, and they were trying to explain something called a diffused axonal injury. A diffused axonal injury, or DAI, is a type of traumatic brain injury. It represents the shearing or tearing of the brain's nerve fibers (or axons). It happens when trauma causes the brain to shift inside the skull. These axons are responsible for carrying the electrical impulses between the brain and the rest of the body. They basically control every function of your body (and I mean *every* function). They grade a DAI on a scale from 1 to 3, with 3 being the most severe. To get to a grade 3, you had to have damage to the brain stem.

Layla was a 3.

At the time, we couldn't really understand what they were saying. They strongly encouraged that we did not Google it. If we did, we'd find that her injury had a 44% fatality rate and actually surviving didn't seem much better. Typically, surviving meant you remained unconscious, very similar to the state she was in now. Best case scenario, she would be severely disabled.

The timing of their news wasn't ideal. My son had just told me he was downstairs checking in through security. I wanted a little time to grieve this news without alarming him. I wanted to meet him outside the unit to have a chance to prepare him. I wanted to be able to give him my absolute attention and help him process the scene. I was able to reach him just steps before he walked into the room. He picked me right up off my feet and wrapped me in a hug in the middle of the ICU. Right then, I knew I'd been wrong: The timing was perfect. I really needed that hug. For the moment, I would put Layla's prognosis away and support our son.

He walked into the room, and I watched his expression take everything in. He was frozen at her bedside, staring at his little sister like he was in a trance. I can only imagine the thoughts running through his mind. He remained this way quite a while. I knew he needed to process this in his own way, so I just stood with him waiting to be needed. I wished I could make this better. Watching the siblings suffer was almost worse than watching Layla. They had to feel every bit of this. They were living the nightmare while she slept.

Eventually I convinced him to grab a pizza in the café downstairs. I knew he hadn't eaten yet, and it had been a while since we had a pizza date. His senior year of high school, he would get out early at 11:30. I would pick him up, and we would grab a slice of pizza. Pizza reviews had become our thing, and it was a fun way to bond. We would review and rank the pizza and try finding new places to score. I never imagined we would be reviewing hospital pizza, but here we were. He ate an entire pie to himself before returning to the room to fall asleep in our little chair bed. He looked so big in that thing, his legs hanging off the bottom. He was out cold and stayed that way for hours. Every time a nurse popped in, they would giggle at the huge man child I had tucked in my tiny chair bed.

A part of me was enjoying this. It was not typical family time, but we were together. Silver lining, right? I was so preoccupied with having him there that I had almost forgotten about the news from earlier. I was glad I had been wrong about wanting him to visit; it ended up being such a gift on such a difficult day.

43

The next day we would be meeting with the neurosurgeon for more explanation about the MRI and what this meant for her future days. I hated sharing bad news with the world. I knew how people had hope for her. I had hope for her, too.

There was no point in getting into specifics until we knew more so I kept it light that night.

> *I'm sorry I'm not responding. I see your texts, emails, and comments though. I just don't know how to say it out loud sometimes, and it's painful to share that I don't have the good news we all want. Every day I'm hoping there's a miracle, and I can share that instead. MRI results were as we feared. The trauma team delivered the blow this morning. Still waiting on neuro before I post what that means. Meantime, keep praying, harder please. I don't believe this is over; I refuse to. Miracles happen every day. God is in control, not us and not those doctors.*

Day 8: Sunday, May 29th

Jeremiah and I had been taking turns staying nights with her. I had stayed home the night before to spend some time with our son before he had to leave. My family had taken Cali on a trip, and my husband's aunt and uncle were arriving from Georgia later that afternoon.

Mary Jane and Kerry may have been his blood, but they were very near and dear to my heart. Mary Jane was someone I often called for guidance and advice, like a mother, and she always treated me like one of her own. Layla's middle name was Jane because of her, and the two of them always shared their own special bond. I was looking forward to their arrival; I knew they would bring comfort with their presence.

I met them in the hallway and fell into Mary Jane's arms. Then, I led them to see Layla. Part of us was desensitized to Layla's appearance, but we were always reminded how bad she looked each time a new person saw her. Seeing Layla in that state had a way of leveling even the strongest person. It was never easy to witness. I always felt a bit of guilt about it, as if I had caused them that pain in some way. This visit was a particularly tough one. I modeled a lot of my current behaviors after these two and trusted their judgement. Seeing their reaction was another confirmation for me that this was bad. After their initial tears, they settled at her bedside to talk and pray with her. I loved observing their interactions with Layla. Most visitors didn't really engage with her, not that I blamed them. She was hard to look at in that state, and it's not like she would respond to them anyway. But Mary Jane and Kerry just dove in and loved on her in the same manner we did. They treated her as if she was still the girl they knew, and I was sure Layla would appreciate that.

Later, they would return home with me to inventory the mess and see how they could help me get it together. Laundry seemed to be my biggest challenge, mostly Layla's. It was one of the reminders of her scattered all over the house and in baskets piled high in her room. I was still struggling to enter that room. Last time I was in there I picked up the hat she had taken from her dad at lunch the day before the accident and broke down. That hat represented the past to me; we had no idea our whole world would change just 24 hours after she took it. So, I decided it was best to stay out of there, and let Mary Jane handle that part for me.

From the start of this unexpected journey, there were a lot of coincidences—events timed perfectly. At least that's what I thought the first few times these things happened. Eventually I realized there can only be so many "coincidences" before you admit there's more to the story. No one is that lucky! Clearly, there was a higher power taking care of the little details for us.

It started with that lucky parking spot, then meeting Kathleen. Kathleen would periodically come by and check on us, and the entire ICU floor treated us like VIP because of her. Earlier that morning, she quietly mentioned something to me that I still hadn't figured out.

"Get her to The Shepherd Center," she said.

When I asked what that meant, she told me it was a hospital in Georgia. I was confused because we were already at a hospital. Why would I need to go to a different one? And why Georgia? I lived in Florida; Georgia was a whole state away! But a few hours later when the neurosurgeon came by to talk about Layla's MRI, it started to make sense. He explained what the next few weeks would look like for our girl. Layla would need tracheotomy surgery, her jaw wired, and a stomach peg put in (not that any of that made sense to us). If she weathered all these things and remained stable, their work was done. She would then need to be transferred to another facility in the hopes they could rehab her and train us for her future care. We were completely ignorant this was how it all worked, so much so that I almost felt offended they wanted us to leave. I was still hoping they would fix her right here and right now. I couldn't even picture how you could transport someone in her condition!

I had my work cut out for me. I felt like everything was shifting. Our little ICU room was sad, but it was peaceful and became comfortable in many ways. Now, they were talking about all these crazy surgeries and moving her somewhere else. I was still very confused about what Shepherd Center even was and why Kathleen would have suggested a place so far when I found a list of rehabs that were much closer. Surely she had to know that! She had to know how hard moving Layla a full state away had to be!

That night I was talking with Mary Jane when another one of those "coincidences" happened. Her daughter, Jessica, needed to relay a message to me. One of Jessica's friends, Corrie, had been following our story through social media. Corrie worked at the Shepherd Center and immediately knew Layla needed a place like it. She understood the urgency of the situation and offered to help us facilitate and guide us in it. Mary Jane and Jessica understood as little as I did, so to all of us, the idea seemed unrealistic.

That is until I started researching.

Yes, there were rehabs closer to home, but Layla needed a miracle. Layla needed the best brain rehab out there. She didn't need good; she needed great. And the great ones were nowhere near us! It became clear that Shepherd Center was one of the best based on the information I found online. This place really seemed magical. It also seemed very hard to get into.

I needed a plan.

What if I could get in?
What if this Corrie girl could make that happen?
What if I could get my insurance to cover this?

Could I realistically move to Georgia for an uncertain amount of time?

Could I bring Cali?

Mary Jane has three daughters (well, four if you include me), and they all live in the vicinity of the Shepherd Center. When we realized this was the place Layla needed to be, she got right to work. She reached out to her girls, and everyone was instantly on board. They were willing to take turns with Cali, give us a place to stay, and support our family during the hardest part of this journey. Not only were they willing, they were excited to do it. Their willingness helped me get excited, too. The idea of brain rehab didn't seem so bad this way. We would be surrounded by family who very clearly loved us. Maybe this would be like an adventure.

To say I wasn't scared would be a lie. This whole thing was scary. So many pieces would have to fall into place, but with their support and guidance, it felt somehow possible. It was time to call Corrie and tell the world the news.

I've rewritten this 57 times so bear with me. I'm trying to put a positive spin on this as much as possible. The MRI was pretty much what we feared from the beginning. Severe brain shearing and damage to the brain stem. There's not much more the hospital can do for her, and she will need to be relocated in the next few weeks. There are a few surgeries she must undergo first to make transition easier, and she must remain stable. The positive is she's strong, vitals are strong, but she has a long way to go. The options for facilities are nowhere near my home so it looks like I'll be temporarily moving. I don't know where yet. It will depend on which one we get into and how my insurance works. We have to somehow figure out how to tell our 10-year-old this. It hurts. I'm grieving the loss of my old life that was pulled out from under me so fast. I'm nervous how I'm going to manage taking care of both of my daughters in a new place. I'm worried about my job. I'm worried about Jeremiah remaining home with the dogs so he can continue working and try his best not to think about his daughters being very far away. (Friends, please make sure he's fed!) This is hands down the hardest thing we've ever done, and there are still a ton of uncertainties of what it will look like, so, needing prayers the place I want to go will be an option. When this whole nightmare began, I begged God just to let her live. She sustained injuries that should have killed her, and her heart still beats. Jeremiah put it best today while I fell apart in that room. He said "Ali, we thought she died that day, and if she did, we'd be begging for these last moments with her." She's still in there, she's still healing, and she's still fighting. I am just continuing to pray and keeping faith God is repairing every cell in her brain as we speak. As much as I struggle at times to understand why this is happening to us, I know most of my struggles have had really pretty endings. So, I'm asking God for that, just let this be a really magical pretty ending and carry us through it. Keep praying, because we are going to need it a little while longer. Thank you as always for such an outpour of love for our Layla and our family.

Day 9: Monday, May 30th

We were very cautious about what visitors we allowed to see Layla. I constantly questioned what she would want. Would she be okay with people seeing her in this condition? A part of me really believed she was going to fully recover and would want to know all the details. I didn't want her to get upset with me about who I let in. There had been a small handful of close friends, and of course, we allowed family. I wanted to give people closure—the ones I knew would need it—but visitors were difficult for us. We felt their pain. Each new visitor brought with them another wave of sadness. Layla always loved an audience, but did this count?

I documented as much as I could with notes. I took pictures and videos every day, and the Facebook page had a pretty good timeline she could use later to recount the entire thing. I had the feeling that, if she woke up, she'd want to know it all. I really did my best to stay two steps ahead of her progress. I even joined a few online support groups for survivors, so I could familiarize myself with the challenges she could have later. I didn't really dig into the injury itself, and I didn't google the DAI thing. I acted as if she was going to recover and prepared myself for that.

I knew enough though. I knew there was a strong possibility I would end up with a severely handicapped daughter. I knew she potentially wouldn't speak or walk again. I tried to embrace this idea. Because I also knew we would somehow make the best of it. I had always had a soft spot for people with disabilities, and now, part of me wondered if this was why. Maybe I was meant for this all along.

I got in touch with Corrie, and instantly, I loved her. She was a wealth of information when it came to brain injuries. She worked with them all day every day. I was constantly bouncing things off her, and she was constantly talking me off the ledge. She had notified admissions at Shepherd about us and had me in direct contact with one of their case managers. Once again, I felt like a VIP. Just like Kathleen, Corrie was clearing a path for us and making a bad situation feel a little easier. And just like Kathleen, Corrie was a stranger to us before this. They didn't have to help us the way they did, and yet, they both signed up for it. It's a gift I'll never forget.

As Layla's story spread, people started connecting me to anyone they thought could help us. It was hard to get through all the emails sometimes because there were so many coming in every day. Many of those connections were people who had survived a brain injury or their caretakers. One story in the bunch stood out to me. It was a woman named Fio. She had been in an accident and suffered an injury like Layla's. She was given a similar prognosis and made an impressive recovery. Several different friends shared her story with me and were urging me to connect with her. That day, Fio commented on the page. Her words were something I would take with us through our whole journey. She encouraged me to speak life into Layla. She shared the same affirmations her sister would speak over her.

You are safe,
you are protected,
you are loved,
and you are healed.

These became the words I repeated throughout the day over Layla. They're words I still speak over her today.

Layla's eyelids started fluttering that day, not quite opening, but still, there was movement. We celebrated everything at that point, and we were anxious to see those blue eyes again someday. There was still no pain response, so that day, a nurse tried something different. She tickled the bottom of Layla's left foot. It took a few tries, but eventually, Layla slightly wiggled her foot. It wasn't as dramatic as she normally would have done it. After all, she hated her feet touched. Still, she was responding, and seeing that little movement was a great way to end the day.

Taking every day as it comes, and I'm happy to say today felt a little brighter. Nothing monumental as far as what doctors call progress, but she started moving her eyelids today and ever so slightly opening those pretty blue eyes. (And I mean hardly at all, but who cares?) Just seeing them move was so amazing. Still no "deliberate" movements or whatever they call it, but I don't care. She wasn't doing that yesterday, so I'm going to celebrate it. I think we are becoming more desensitized to seeing her like this, so it gets a little easier each day. Don't get me wrong, I cry, A LOT, but today, I just enjoyed being near her. Playing her music, praying with her, talking to her, reading her the sweet messages everyone sends, giving her scratches. Today I just felt peace and enjoyed my girl. Layla never sat still so it was something new for both of us. Working on our new normal, which changes daily. Tomorrow is a bit crazier. She has 2 surgeries scheduled, but they don't tell us the time. I'm not excited about it, but I know it's just getting her closer to healing. I learned so much about the brain and brain injuries these last days, literally tons of doctors daily giving us this information and all with different opinions. The only consistent thing I keep hearing is we don't know much about the brain and how complex it is, and every case is different, and there's no rule book, etc. So, I'm going to continue to trust God instead and wait for Layla to show them who the REAL healer is. Keep sending up those prayers and as always THANK YOU for being a part of this.

Day 10: Tuesday, May 31st

Today was a big day.

Layla needed three surgeries before we could relocate her. Today, they would be doing the tracheotomy and wiring her jaw. Her jaw was broken in several places, and she was having some sort of plates installed. The tracheotomy was going to replace the intubation. I was really struggling with that one. Up until that moment, there was a tube in her mouth going down into her lungs delivering oxygen. This wasn't meant to be a long-term thing, and her situation was starting to look long term. Currently, that tube was running through her vocal cords, which can cause issues later. Now they were going to make an incision in her throat and directly into her windpipe where a plastic device would be secured on the outside. A hose would run from the device to the ventilator to help her breathe. It's the same idea as what she had before, only this felt more permanent. I had seen people with trachs on TV before. I never understood or even thought about why they needed them. Now, I unfortunately understood it all too well.

They rarely took Layla out of that room, maybe two other times for a scan since we'd arrived. Those only took 20 minutes, but we'd been prepared that this would take much longer. They said to expect it to take at least three hours. Jeremiah and I would have to find something to occupy ourselves. I had recently gotten a new car that had all the bells and whistles. One of those fancy features? Massagers in the seats. When

I got the car, I thought it was such an excessive feature. Why would you need a massage in the car?

That day, I understood it completely.

We were both exhausted and sore from sleeping in that chair night after night. So, I suggested we go sit in the car and put that thing to work! I figured we could pretend we were at a spa. Silly, maybe, but life in the ICU makes anything outside of it feel like a luxury. The two of us hung out in the car for a while until we realized we hadn't eaten that day. I ordered from one of those handy food delivery services, and we decided to eat in the cafeteria for a change of scenery. There we sat by a window, eating burgers and fries when I just started giggling. It occurred to me that we were on a date: massages and dinner. It was nothing like our usual dates, but here we were, improvising and going with it. It was clear our life was going to look different from then on, so why not try to make it entertaining?

"Hot date," I said to him still giggling away. Jeremiah is accustomed to this side of me. I knew he enjoyed my laughs that day, even if he repeatedly shook his head and said I was crazy.

When we were done, we decided to go upstairs and wait for our girl. I'm grateful Jeremiah was with me for this moment. Seeing her again was a lot to take in. I could hardly look at the thing coming out of her neck, yet I was mesmerized by her beautiful face. I hadn't seen her face in so long. I did my best to keep it together while my husband kept me calm, repeating the benefits of this thing. I know it was hard for him, too; he was just choosing to ease my pain over his own. I knew the sacrifice he was making for me. It wouldn't be the first time he put me before himself, but it had been a long time since I really thought about it. I left him with Layla that night and drove home, soaked in gratitude for a successful day. That feeling only grew when Jeremiah texted me about 15 minutes after I left with big news.

Layla had opened her eyes.

We've been in that room for 10 days now. Strangely, it's gotten kind of normal, almost comfortable. I know how to get around the hospital when I need stuff, I know most of the nurses and doctors now, the sounds of all the machines aren't as scary to me anymore. I have a whole new respect for nurses and especially the ICU ones. We are on the pediatric floor, so we see a lot of parents doing the same things we are: crying, praying, waiting. We all look kind of desperate. The nurses are usually a lot more optimistic than the doctors, and most of them have told me, "Don't lose hope, we see miracles every day." Those words mean so much sometimes. It really takes special people to do that job, and I'm excited for the day Layla can march into that unit and thank them. Anyways, she had a great day again. She did more of that eye thing I like, had physical therapy, and was sent to surgery around 3:00. It took about three and a half hours. The tracheotomy was done first, then she had jaw surgery. Sounds awful, but she handled it like a champ. The tracheotomy took me time to process and have peace with, but now I can see her beautiful face and lips. No more tubes and tape everywhere; it was so good to see that face. Plus, the trach is much safer for her and will help her heal faster (thank you nurses and friends for helping me accept that). Jaw surgery was much easier than originally anticipated. She only needed one metal plate instead of two (jaw is broken in 2 places), and she is wired shut for about a month. Sounds like a rough day but it really was little miracles. Day 1 I didn't think we'd get to this point, not sure doctors even did, and here we are. I am excited for a big week; I have a feeling she's going to show off a little. I'm so grateful, almost giddy about seeing her face. I really missed that face. I'm so grateful she's still with us. I'm so grateful those two surgeries are done. I'm just so grateful she keeps fighting, and we're still in this. I'm so grateful for amazing friends, and support, and doors being opened as we need them. I am just SOOOO GRATEFUL.

Day 11: Wednesday, June 1ˢᵗ

Her eyes opening was not what we expected it would be. Her usual bright blue eyes looked like the light was gone in them. They didn't move either. She had a blank expression, like she was staring ahead at nothing. They weren't open all the time. Usually, they were shut. It would startle me sometimes when I'd glance over to see her empty eyes. It was almost easier when her eyes were closed. This didn't feel like Layla at all. This was our daughter, but her spirit was not present. There seemed to be no life in this girl that had taken over Layla's body. One of the milestones she needed to reach is called tracking, which is basically following objects with her eyes. I would walk from one side of the bed to the other calling her name and asking her to look at me. I definitely got my steps in that day, but Layla just stared straight ahead into nothing. It was a new skill, so I told myself she needed time to adjust. I mean, it had been a long time since she used those eyes.

Each day, Layla's ventilator support was gradually being reduced. She seemed to be handling this part well. If she failed to breathe strong enough, an alarm would go off, and the machine knew to kick on and assist. The nurses didn't seem too alarmed by this sound, but we were. That alarm would send us into a full panic. Sometimes Jeremiah would even give her a nudge when it happened, almost trying to encourage her to keep breathing. That morning, they turned the pressure all the way off. We questioned the nurses when they did this, like we were the ones who did this for a living and not them. To us, it just seemed scary. What if

56

she didn't breathe? They assured us it was safe, and the machine would assist if needed. Of course, we trusted them, and of course, Layla did the work.

Previously, when they would come in for physical therapy, there wasn't much involved. It was mostly bending her limbs in mechanical-like movements. We would mimic their exercises afterwards; we figured it was like extra practice. Spasticity, an uncontrollable tightening of the muscles, is very common after a brain injury. Typically, you recognize it in the hands first. They had these rolled up towels in her hands to prevent her from clenching her fists. We called them her dumbbells and were always messing with them. It gave us something to do. Foot drop was another new term we learned, too. It was also common after TBI. It looks just like it sounds. Picture the top of your foot dropping toward the ground when laying down. It's a disruption in the nervous system and the muscles that typically tell your feet to lift, especially after lying still that long. To help, they brought in these inflatable shoes that kept her feet in the correct position. They were open at the top, so we could see her toes. We called them her moon boots (we had nicknames for everything). They plugged them into a little generator at the foot of her bed and vibrated to keep her blood flowing. She had a similar contraption on her legs.

Now that she'd had those surgeries, they were able to start more intense physical therapies. I remember laughing inside when they told us that. I thought physical therapy would require the ability to actually move! I needed physical therapy for an injury once. They had me on stair machines and treadmills, and there were squats involved. There was no way Layla was doing any of that. Slow motion blinking seemed to be the only moving she could do. She had been lying flat for eleven days. Every two hours they would come in and turn her, but it was more like a tilt. They used these foam wedges angled under her body. It was explained to us that they were preventing pressure wounds or bed sores. I always imagined bed sores were caused from days or weeks of lying there, but I was wrong. They can happen with just 2-3 hours of cutting off blood flow to the skin. They are nasty little problems that can become very serious, a lesson we would learn later down the road.

As unbelievable as it seemed to me, physical therapy arrived to get to work on our girl. They rolled a rectangular table with black straps running across it in with them. There wasn't a lot of space in that room, so they fit the table between our sleeping chair and Layla's bed. The therapists moved Layla onto the table using a lift sheet. Once she was on the table, they began securing the straps. This funny looking table was called a tilt table. They were going to use it to slowly stand her upright and put some pressure on her feet and ankles. They wanted to see how she handled it. Then, they would raise the table a little more each time and wait to see what happened. They were watching to see how the different positions affected her heart rate and blood pressure. She reminded me of Frankenstein attached to that thing—being raised up with all the wires and tubes still attached to her and eyes still closed. Back then I wasn't entirely sure of the purpose behind all this, but the therapists seemed pleased with Layla's performance. She had passed another one of their tests, which meant tomorrow they would try something harder.

This was a very productive day. They had told us things would go backwards sometimes and to expect setbacks. Not today though. Today she was showing off. I would get carried away with the optimism sometimes. Jeremiah would try to keep me even keeled, but on days like this one, it was useless. I was bouncing off the walls. I wanted to tell the world what our girl did. This was a proud moment.

She had a really busy day. They started her on more aggressive physical therapy, which is both keeping her muscles loose and helping stimulate senses, and they let us play her favorite music during it. Layla is a radio hog and loves music. She will let me request a song here and there, but mostly, she takes over radio controls, and she likes it loud! Anyone whose car she's been in knows what I'm talking about. We play a lot of music in the room for her, and I can't wait till she can wake up

58

and complain about my music choices. This morning, they also turned down the support for her breathing. She's still technically on a ventilator as back up if needed, but she is officially breathing on her own with assistance. It's a little terrifying when they just shut it off at first and trust her to do the work. But she showed up and did it, you'd think I'd know better than to ever bet against Layla. In the beginning of this the doctors said we had to take it minute by minute, then it was hour by hour. She keeps fighting and doing better, so now, it's day by day. She amazes us and the doctors every day. No doubt in my mind from the prayers and love. Layla's love language is physical touch. She loves holding hands and needs daily hugs, and I can't wait for that. For today, I'm celebrating these little red lines because this girl can breathe!

Day 12: Thursday, June 2nd

Being overly optimistic was dangerous for me sometimes. I would get addicted to the high of good news. I expected things were just going to keep going up, and Layla would keep doing new things. Some days it wasn't like that, and that's when I would crash. Some days we had to be content for just another day with her. They warned us we would have setbacks. They told us it was a marathon, and they never promised we would get any more progress. You really had to just be in that day and not expect anything more. That is not an easy thing for a girl with no patience. I wanted to know how this was going to end. I wanted to start our new life with whatever version of Layla we got to keep. I wasn't as afraid of losing her anymore, even though it was definitely still possible. I had moved on to the next step in my brain, and I was ready to get to work.

What is our life going to be like?
How can I train for this?

I remembered how I read all these parenting books when I was pregnant. I thought that, with enough help, I could master being a mom. This was the same, except this was something I couldn't plan for. There isn't much you can read or learn because no two brain injuries are the same. There was only so much I could do to mentally and emotionally prepare for the road ahead because that road was mostly unknown.

Physical therapy had something new planned that day. They would sit her upright on the edge of the bed with her feet hanging off the side. They wanted her to engage her core and possibly support her head. She couldn't do any of it; she just sat there like a rag doll. There was a therapist behind her supporting her neck and back while another stabilized her from the front. Her therapists didn't seem upset about it, but I certainly was.

I wanted more.
I wanted another step forward.
I *needed* another step forward.

We were still trying to get her to track movements or move her fingers and toes on command. Doctors wanted to see "deliberate" movements. For some reason I felt like we were up against a clock, and it seemed as if we were losing. Jeremiah said I was trying to win a marathon in the first mile. I was panicking about the time going by. She still didn't seem to be in there. It was like someone had highjacked my daughter's body, and she was trapped somewhere deep inside. I feared she'd be trapped like this forever. I couldn't stop thinking about how much she would hate this, and eventually, I started to spiral. I needed some advice. I needed someone to tell me straight. So, I decided to text Corrie.

Me: I know I keep asking you, but I have moments of such fear. It's day 12. They switched her to a trach collar today, but she still isn't doing any deliberate movements or tracking with her eyes. Is it possible she still needs time? Or is she moving slower than average?

Corrie: It's totally OK. She just needs more time. Right now, what you will see is fewer medical issues and overall, more stability. But it's OK that she's not what we would consider awake yet. The brain takes time.

Me: So, this isn't a bad sign? Like she won't be stuck like this forever? Sorry, for some reason I'm falling apart today.

Corrie: I can't tell you that she's going to wake up right now. Sometimes people do wind up in minimally conscious states and don't wake up to the point where they can interact and talk. You're in an "only time will tell." Without seeing her scans, it's hard to know. Even seeing

61

her scans only tells someone what could happen based on science. We know what can happen based on faith. You're allowed to fall apart; it's more concerning if you don't. Trust your doctors, but trust your momma gut, too, and trust Jesus.

I can tell you based on experience I have spent months attempting to wake someone up, and he went home minimally conscious, but he came back awake and walking. I've also spent months attempting to wake someone up, and she went home and is still minimally conscious, but we prepared her family, and they have created the sweetest life around her. It's hard, it's sad. Everything changed 12 days ago. You're allowed to mourn that, but you do have to keep looking forward too. If that makes sense.

Me: I know she wouldn't want to live like this. It looks like torture.

Corrie: I understand that. Are they asking about that?

Me: No, these are just my crazy thoughts.

Corrie: Every single day I have those thoughts. Are you prepared for some hard information to hear?

Me: Yea, I suppose

Corrie: Here's the thing. After the accident, they saved her life. We've gotten really good at saving people. That in itself, can be a good thing or bad thing. Initially all you want is for your person to live. Every little thing is a miracle, then, all of a sudden, she's stable. The concern about whether she will live or not is gone, and you start thinking, "What kind of life is she going to have?" And now you spiral that way. This is now out of your hands unless you choose to stop feeding her. She's breathing on her own. She's slowly waking up. We have no idea what her future holds, and it's easy to look at her and think she wouldn't want this. It's terrifying, but it's 12 days in and a lot less terrifying looking than before, right?

62

Me: Yes, true.

Corrie: No one knows more than you what the right decision is for her, but don't let fear make it for you. I feel like every day y'all send me something. It's one more thing she's doing, even if it's not intentional.

Me: So, there's still hope? Do you often see this turn out right, moving at her slow progression? I don't even know if this is considered slow.

Corrie: This isn't slow progression, Ali, I promise.

Me: Seems it.

Corrie: It's slow for you, but it's not slow for her.

Me: OK. I trust you. That actually gives me peace.

Corrie: What I hope is wherever she goes (hopefully Shepherd, selfishly), because it will be a neuro rehab center, we can see more progression with medication changes, and the right therapies, but it's still going to be slow to you. There will never be a point where she's getting better fast enough for y'all.

Me: I can see that. I know I'm rushing because I'm anxious.

Corrie: And that's OK too, parents are allowed to be a little crazy.

Me: Then I just keep praying.

Corrie: You can ask me all the questions, if I don't know the answer, I'll ask someone else.

Me: Thank you so much, you have truly been such help.

That was one of many conversations like that. She had a great way of explaining things to me. She didn't sugarcoat it, but she was tender at the same time. I had spells where I felt manic. I was so worried about her future. I was worried about *our* futures. This was going to impact the whole family in some way. I had confidence I could take care of her and love her just the same. This wasn't about that; this was about what Layla would want. It's not like she could tell me. I was worried she would never be able to. I wanted her to have a voice in this.

Some days I just needed to fall apart and then regroup.
Tomorrow would be a new day.

During all this, someone told me it's ok to cry out to God and say I'm not ok, and I can't do this. Today has been one of those kinds of days. I'm thankful Layla is still stable, thankful she's breathing on her own, thankful for another day with her. I'm doing my best to focus on those things. But this is really hard. There are so many unknowns and a ton of waiting. Plus, the unknowns of what her future looks like. I'm thankful for the plethora of resources I've been given and people to reach out to, even late at night. I want to be able to update everyone on something new and amazing she did every day, but it's just not how this works and I'm going to need some blind faith and a lot of patience. So, for today, her just being with us was the amazing news I have. I know our God is bigger than all this and works in his perfect timing. I keep being told we are just starting a marathon, so I'm going to need those prayers a while longer. As always, thank you for all the support and love.

Day 13: Friday, June 3rd

I woke up determined to make today a good one.

I was going to keep doubt out of my mind and just surrender. I would be better for Layla; I would be patient. Jeremiah and I never seemed to have our good days on the same days, which worked out perfectly. We could take turns being strong. It was like partnering in a dance. When one of us was weak, the other could lead. Being strong is exhausting, so it was nice to get a break and be able to lean on the other one.

That day, however, we were both on the same page.

When I arrived in the ICU that morning, I noticed an empty bed still in the packaging at the front of the unit. That bed was for Layla. Kathleen had ordered an upgrade for her (another one of those VIP perks). Just the sight of the new bed somehow made the day feel better than the one before. This bed would also act as a tilt table for her therapy sessions, so it had a lot of new features to figure out. It reminded me of that new car I had downstairs. That thing had way too many buttons and options for me. Every time I tried to do something simple like listen to the radio, I'd end up hitting all the wrong stuff. I usually had to call Jeremiah to help me undo whatever it was I'd just done. Once, I even drove miles with the parking brake on. But honestly, in my defense, why would a parking brake be such a little button? It's supposed to be big, and obvious, and clearly marked that it shouldn't be touched unless there was an emergency. Needless to say, there was no way I was going to mess with the buttons on her bed or her machines. That, of course, was more Jeremiah's area.

Her room was busy that morning. They were getting her new bed set up, and we were able to get some more living space. She had successfully gone days without needing the ventilator assistance, so that big bulky machine was getting rolled out of her room. Jeremiah had named it R2Vent2, and now, he was finally leaving. She had officially graduated to a trach collar. It was also a lot quieter in the room without the ventilator. The best part? This all meant our girl was mostly breathing on her own. This was a big step in the right direction.

I didn't really know what the next phase would be because I'd promised myself I would try to just stay in the day. The therapy team came to practice standing Layla up again. This time, they would do it with the help of her new bed. They stood her a little more upright than last time, and like last time, she tolerated it great. We were two for two today. Just when we thought it couldn't get any better, our case manager walked in with the news we'd been praying for: Our insurance had approved us to go to Shepherd Center. They had a bed waiting for us. Not just any bed, this was the *only* bed available.

The only bed in the entire center would go to our Layla. Coincidence? I didn't think so.

I don't think we realized we had been holding our breath for days waiting on this news. We could both finally exhale and move on to the next leg of this journey. We had no idea how the details would work, and honestly, we didn't care.

We were going to move to Georgia to save our daughter.

I was spending the night with Layla that night, and Jeremiah was going home to Cali. Cali had been channeling some of her emotions through music lately. She borrowed a guitar her brother left behind and was learning to play via the Internet. Jeremiah is more of the music guy in our house, so he was going to take her to the music store to purchase a guitar her size. It was adorable actually. He was sending me videos and pictures of the two of them sampling the guitars and picking up dinner.

It was nice seeing her smile. She had really been struggling lately. She no longer wanted to hang out with her friends and preferred only a select few of mine. Jenna and Nicole seemed to be her favorites. They both also lived on our street, and Cali had gotten very attached to staying home or close by it (and subsequently, close by them).

Only now, I was going to move her to Georgia.

To this day I don't understand why Cali turned out to be excited about it, but in reality, she was very excited. I knew she loved our family there, but visiting and moving are two different things. She knew she would likely start school in the fall in Georgia and be the new kid in a new place. That alone I thought would terrify her, but she took it all in stride. Maybe her focus was just like ours: We were going to save her sister.

My mood was boosted by this news, I took to the Facebook page to share the update.

> *Layla has always wanted to move to the country. I don't even know if she understood what that meant because the girl would break down without her Starbucks and malls. A few days ago, I told you she will need to be moved to a long-term facility soon. Today I got the call: The facility we wanted is going to take her. It wasn't as easy as a phone call, and a lot of pieces had to fall into place, thanks to a few very helpful friends and family. Plus, Layla had to do her part. So, she is getting her wish and will be moving to Georgia (not sure that even counts as the country!). We have five sleeps before we relocate our life. We have to figure out how she gets there. I learned all about air ambulances today. The facility is The Shepherd Center in Atlanta, and it's the best in country, or so I've been told. I have peace about it. From the minute I knew this was happening, I knew it had to be there. We have an incredible support team there who will be taking us in and helping with Cali. I was so scared to tell Cali about leaving. She's been struggling a lot lately and I was bracing myself for more tears. Well, there were tears followed by a huge hug and thanking me for doing this. I didn't see that coming. So, our new adventure begins potentially Wednesday. God is good.*

That night, I was getting my little bed prepared for the night. The chair we slept in converted to a bed with a few easy steps (well, easy to some). I couldn't figure it out. Usually, Jeremiah left it open for me for this exact reason. It seemed stuck, or jammed, or maybe I'd messed it up like the buttons in my car. Finally, I gave up and called him. I could have scripted how this call was going to go. He would try explaining it, and I wouldn't understand. My brain just doesn't speak mechanically. I was over it. He urged me to go ask for help, but I was embarrassed, so I lied and told him I would. A few moments later, a nurse came in to help. Jeremiah had called the nurse's station and asked them to come assist me. He knew I wouldn't ask for help. This is the side of him I originally fell in love with—the boy who takes care of me even when I say I don't need it. Plus, he's pretty good at fixing all the stuff I break.

Each day we became more comfortable handling Layla. We had been studying nurses and therapists for almost two weeks at that point. We wanted to learn from them so we could help with her care. We tried to be helpful while still staying out of their way. In a sense, we were a team. We could handle a few of the grooming tasks, like brushing her hair, applying lotion or ChapStick, massaging her hands and feet—the minor things. One of my friends had brought me essential oils and a diffuser. We had the diffuser going 24/7 in that room. We also rubbed the oils on her temples and feet every two hours. This was my kind of medicine. I am a believer in the benefits of that stuff, and I wanted any advantage possible to help Layla. Bonus: Her room smelled fantastic, and the nurses loved it.

It was about 9:00 pm by then. I was applying oils to Layla's feet like every other night when something different happened: Her toes started wiggling. There had been times when she did move, but it was never like this. This was real movement.

I froze and pulled my hands back.
Did I really see that?

"Layla," I said boldly, "Can you wiggle your toes again?"

Right on command, she did it.

I waited a few moments in disbelief before I asked again, and once again, she did it. I moved over to her side and grabbed her left hand.

"Layla," I said again, "Can you move your hand?"

Her hand started moving immediately in response.

Layla could hear me!
These were deliberate movements!
She was moving on command!

I needed a doctor to see this, put it in her chart, stamp her TBI passport—anything they had to do to document this progress. I knew there were no doctors making the rounds that late, so I grabbed my phone and began recording. I was afraid she wouldn't do it the next day. I was afraid her dad wouldn't get to witness this. I knew this would mean as much to him as it did to me. This was what we had been waiting for— some sign she was in there, some sign she could hear us. I was going to wait until Jeremiah arrived the next day and surprise him in person, but I couldn't keep it in. So, I sent him the videos.

Jeremiah: She's going to make a full recovery babe, I know it. You have to keep the faith.

Me: I'm sorry about yesterday. I was struggling.

Jeremiah: I know it's tough right now, but I need you to keep the faith. You have a gift, Ali, and strength like no other woman I know.

That boy knew exactly what to say. It was encouraging to hear him say I was strong, mostly because I didn't feel strong. My childhood had made me resilient, yes, but I wasn't always strong. I fell apart a lot, but I

69

always found my way again. Does that count as strong? In his eyes, it certainly did, and that mattered so much to me.

I was up until midnight practicing Layla's new tricks. Finally, I think she fell asleep. It was hard to tell because her eyes were closed a lot regardless of if she was awake or not. She was probably sick of listening to me at that point. I took eleven videos that night before I tucked myself in next to Layla. I was grateful Jeremiah made them fix my bed because finally, I was ready to sleep. I felt so hopeful as my head hit the pillow. This was promising. This had potential. We could find a way to communicate. If she couldn't use her voice, she could use her hands.

I made a decision right then and there. I wouldn't put unrealistic expectations on her. I wanted one thing only and that would be it: I wanted Layla to be able to tell me if she was happy.

I was willing to wait until she could.
If she was happy, we could figure out the rest.

Day 14: Saturday, June 4th

I woke up early thinking the whole thing was a dream. Did Layla really move on command last night? Would she do it again today? Before I could get up and find out, a nurse walked in to check on Layla. They typically did the same routine every few hours, and most of our regular nurses were familiar with what she could and couldn't do. This guy wasn't one of our regulars.

He grabbed her hand and loudly said, "Layla can you squeeze my hand?"

I nervously waited until I heard him praise her for moving on his command. I had my answer. Just like that, I burst into tears. I explained through crying that she had just started doing this last night. He looked at me with confidence and compassion.

"She's going to be fine, Mom," he reassured me.

At his words, I fell apart in the best way possible.

Jeremiah wouldn't be back until later that afternoon, so I had Layla to myself, and now, we had work to do. After I shared the news with Corrie, she gave me some exercises to practice with Layla. Because Corrie is an occupational therapist, sometimes her directions were a little advanced for me. I had to Google most of what she said to translate, but I felt like

I was really getting the tricks of the trade. She was our insider connection willing to train me before we got to Georgia. She told me to give Layla commands without touching her and to give her an absurd amount of time to process those commands. I was to ask her to do the same command three times and be very specific with my requests. She also stressed it was important to let her rest because her brain would fatigue easily. Admittedly, I had a hard time with that one.

Corrie: You're letting her rest, right?

Me: Kinda. They keep giving her meds and she falls asleep on me sometimes.

Corrie: The brain needs rest, Ali. Don't make me yell at you. Feel free to pester her, but if you mess with her for 15-20 min, then give her time to rest.

Me: Ok, got it.

Me: I played music all day. Is that bad?

Corrie: That's OK. It wasn't trap music, was it?

Me: lol, no.

Me: I was just brushing her hair and hit a knot. She picked her whole arm up!

Corrie: DO NOT start pulling her hair!

Corrie was funny. She was fluent in sarcasm, and I appreciated that. Humor is typically how I cope with most scenarios. It's how I got through losing my brother. My friends hated it when I made jokes about it, but to me, it was better than crying all the time. Sometimes you need to laugh at your situation, and in this situation, it felt good to laugh.

72

She was still on a few pain medications, and these made her sleepy, especially the valium. When they gave it to her, she could sleep for hours. I had to practice with her in between those little naps. That day, we focused on thumbs up. However, I realized quickly that it wasn't working, so I started asking her just to pick her hand up. I could see how difficult any movement was for her and how much energy it took out of her to even try. Her processing time had a delay, and her movements were really slow, but knowing she could hear me was huge. She still wasn't tracking, but she was trying. Sometimes I could get her to move her eyes by following the cell phone light, and sometimes her eyes would flicker to a new person who entered the room. She had less of the zombie stare and started making some interesting faces. With her jaw being wired, she was limited on facial expressions, but it looked like she was trying. Before the accident, we would tease Layla about her resting face. She always looked annoyed, and I was always telling her to smile more. She was making a similar expression this day, only more exaggerated. Her scowl made me laugh; *this* was something I expected from her. I started noticing how much stronger she was on the left side. She didn't seem to be able to move the right side much at all. Apparently, that is pretty normal, as one side could be weaker or possibly never wake up after an accident like hers. As usual, we weren't promised anything. Layla would just have to learn to be a lefty for now.

Up until that day, I didn't expect I would be posting pictures of her in that condition. We didn't allow visitors to take them, and while we had a library of images, they were for Layla in case she wanted to see them later. I wanted to respect her privacy and honor her wishes, even if she couldn't tell me exactly what they were. I knew enough to know she wouldn't want certain pictures online. Any mother of a teenager daughter knows that! Every time I posted anything of her in the past, it took multiple tries before she was satisfied with the photo. But this day, I really wanted to share her progress. I felt like our new community of friends and family was a safe place to do it. This was, after all, what we all had been praying for. I felt like they were a part of it, too. Still, I was careful to share only videos of her hands and feet. I had confidence she wouldn't mind that.

I hesitate to post this for 2 reasons. For one I'm trying to be mindful of what Layla would want, as anyone with a teenage daughter knows pictures/videos must be approved before they go up. Second, I don't want to give false hope. There's a lot to brain injury. This is going to take a lot of time and there's zero guarantee she will progress to the next step. Many, many don't. There're 10 levels to get her back to what we'd recognize as the Layla before. She's at a 2 right now. Getting her to a 3 involves a few things she isn't doing YET. Tracking with her eyes and simple movements on command. We spend a ton of time asking her if she can wiggle her toes and fingers, over, and over, and over, and so far, nothing. It can be really disheartening and makes me want to kick and scream. I'm sure you noticed the last few days I was struggling. I put essential oils on her toes and temples every few hours. Last night she moved her toes as I was applying, so I waited and asked her to wiggle again, and she did. She repeated this about 3 times on command. You are always worried it's coincidental because she does move and twitch at times. So, I moved on to her hand and asked her to wiggle her fingers. She did. I again repeated this and every time she did. I started videoing because often she won't do the same thing for the doctors, and they probably think I'm crazy. Anyways I'm sharing one of those videos because it makes my heart so happy.

Day 15: Sunday, June 5th

Layla may have been moving on command, but she was still labeled unconscious. One of the many reasons we chose Shepherd was a specific program they had for our scenario. It's called Disorders of Consciousness. Layla would enter the hospital under that program and be given up to six weeks to wake up, or as they called it, "emerge." If she never emerged, then we would return home with her as is, and Shepherd would provide us with training to care for her needs. Many people go home this way, but even then, not all hope is lost. There is still a chance your person may emerge after returning home, or at least that's what they told us. If Layla was to emerge during the six weeks, they would begin the rehab work there. My insurance would cover 60 days of that rehab. So, if everything went as we hoped, we would be in Georgia at least around three and a half months.

When the therapists arrived today, they handed us a big, white binder. We were about to get a lesson on traumatic brain injury recovery. The binder contained information on something called the Rancho Los Amigos Scale. It's a medical scale used to describe the cognitive and behavioral patterns found in brain injury patients as they recover. The book had ten stages and described what each stage would look like. I loved the idea that we could measure and track her progress, but it was also a reminder of how far she had to go. Layla was a two at the time that binder was placed in my hands. Layla was responding to some things but still minimally awake. There is no set time for how long a person takes to get through each stage, and no promise they will even get to the next one. Once again, we knew nothing concrete. They can describe the stages, but that's about it. Everything about a brain injury is frustrating because there are just so many unknowns. I've never heard doctors say, "We just don't know," as much as we heard it in those early days with Layla. It started to feel pointless even asking questions.

Layla had surgery scheduled for the next morning. She would be getting a stomach PEG, which stands for percutaneous endoscopic gastrostomy. It's basically a feeding tube. Previously they had been feeding Layla through her nose with a tube that ran down into her stomach. Just like being intubated, this is not something that is safe to do long term. Between the tracheotomy and the stomach PEG, her situation seemed very permanent. And just like the tracheotomy, this would be something else we'd have to learn to operate in order to care for her. The tracheotomy was hard to look at. They kept a piece of gauze over the opening, but I caught glimpses time to time. When I did, I felt like I could basically look into her body. The opening had to be suctioned frequently by a respiratory team that came by about every two hours. It was one of our least favorite parts, and we knew it would possibly, eventually become our responsibility. I had no idea what a stomach PEG looked like or how it worked, but it seemed more comfortable than the tube running out of her nose. So, if it helped Layla, then we would manage.

The stomach PEG was her last required surgery before we could leave. She would need to be monitored for 24 hours after the procedure before being cleared to go. Then, Layla would need to be medically flown to Shepherd Center. The hospital case manager gave me a paper with about 75 different companies and informed me I'd have to select one for the transport. I did not feel qualified to be doing this, but then again, I didn't feel qualified to be doing any of the other stuff either. We had a lot of research to do. Between finding an air ambulance and reading the binder given to me earlier, it was going to be a long night.

Rancho Los Amigos. No, it's not a tequila. It's the scale that measures cognitive function of the brain. It's those stages I was

76

talking about. They gave us this binder describing each stage and what to expect. I've decided only to read one stage ahead to prepare and recognize what's coming. It also keeps me present in our moment and dealing best with that. I'm no doctor, but she seems like she's venturing into the third stage. If it wasn't about my daughter's future, I would actually find this stuff interesting instead of scary. I had no idea this is how it works and how complex it can be. My heart really goes out to anyone who has experienced this. It can be really cruel. We are used to cheering for Layla, and she typically dominated anything she did, (except ice skating, she was really bad at that). Now we cheer for her fingers and toes moving. She did perform a lot today. She did the movements on command repeatedly for doctors, and nurses, and basically anyone who requested. The looks on doctors' faces were great; I don't think this was expected given how bad the injury is. Her left side is a lot stronger than her right, but that's normal apparently and can change. She started making some really interesting faces, letting them know she was not happy with them messing with her mouth. That was actually pretty funny and something she did prior. So today, you can say she took more steps forward. Praying for continued progress.

Day 16: Monday, June 6th

Today we would get to see another new area of the hospital: the OR. We were allowed to sit with her before they took her into surgery. You don't get an exact time for these surgeries; they just come in and surprise you. They had already taken her down with Jeremiah when I arrived, so he had to navigate me to them. They only allowed one person in with her, so he gracefully switched to give me some time with Layla. She didn't seem to notice what was going on, but that was normal for her now. This day, it was a blessing. Layla before would have been a wreck about all of this. She had a phobia about needles and any kind of medical procedures. There was only one time before this when she had to be hospitalized. She had a bad habit of grinding her teeth when she slept. Eventually, she ground her teeth down so badly that she exposed nerves and ended up getting an abscess. She needed an IV round of antibiotics, and it took four nurses and myself to hold her down for that. She was only seven then. I couldn't even imagine what that would look like for her now!

I was sitting at her bedside taking everything in and thinking about how far she had come. I thought I noticed Layla's eyes watching me. She typically stared through you; this look was different. Before I could fully absorb it, they came for her, and I was instructed to go wait upstairs. I always hated it when they took her from us.

I returned to the room and joined Jeremiah. I wanted to tackle this air ambulance thing while we had the time. My plan was to start with the first company on the list and work my way down. I figured I would get a good feeling when it was the right company, and hopefully, I wouldn't have to call all 75 of them. Jeremiah laughed when I told him my plan. I did the same thing when we had to hire anyone to fix something in the house. We had recently had our AC replaced, and I had three companies coming out to give us quotes. He warned me not to get too friendly with them and to keep my poker face on. He knew it was pointless telling me that. By the time he came home, I knew the life stories of each of our estimators. I liked to select the company that seemed the most honest with the best story, and I would do the same thing here.

I had only made about four phone calls when they rolled Layla back into the room. I was confused because I knew there was no way the surgery could've happened that fast. Apparently, her surgeon did not operate on pediatrics, a fact that immediately annoyed us. How could that get missed? How could she get all the way down there before someone caught that? Whenever she had surgeries scheduled, they would stop certain medications. I assumed she needed these meds, and now, we did that for nothing. It was frustrating to say the least.

I don't know if it was because of the traveling or the lack of medications, but Layla seemed very alert. Even her eyes looked different. Just like I observed downstairs, she was definitely tracking. Her hand was more active than usual, so I took this opportunity to practice thumbs up. This time, she was able to do it. In some ways, it was like having an infant again. It was almost like getting time back with her as a baby. That was how I explained her state to Cali. She was essentially starting over and would need to relearn everything. After that, Cali would dig through her toy chest and send me to the hospital with the little treasures she'd find for her sister. She didn't understand that Layla couldn't interact with even these simple toys, and I didn't have the heart to tell her. So, I would throw them in my bag and thank her, thinking they would never go to use.

Until today.

One of those toys was a sensory ball. It was squishy with a bumpy texture on the outside. When we placed the ball in Layla's hand, she started squeezing and rolling it in her palm. It was perfect! I was excited to show Cali how her efforts were not in vain. We had a few hours with Layla like that. She was very interactive and felt a little more like our daughter. Tomorrow, they would attempt the surgery again, which pushed our exit to Shepherd back one day. If we were learning anything, it was to expect the unexpected.

Today didn't go as planned in the best way possible. They packed her up and took her down to the OR around 10:00. We were able to sit with her a little before they kicked us out for surgery. I thought I noticed her eyes moving a little, but I'm also staring at her face so long sometimes I think I hallucinate. We went back upstairs and maybe ten minutes later they were bringing her back in. Apparently, the surgeon didn't want to operate on a pediatric case. Blessing in disguise though because I don't want someone cutting her open who isn't confident about doing it. Another plus was she was SUPER awake from all the traveling. I took advantage of this to work with her. For starters she was tracking us with her eyes, like really watching us! Following us all over the room. Watching new people who came into mess with her machines and was picking up her hands a lot. So, I started making thumbs up requests and see for yourself: I think she nailed it. Even gave me a dirty look when I got the hairbrush stuck in her hair. Tomorrow she should have the surgery, and the air ambulance has been secured for her exit. We've loved the 16 days of care at St. Mary's, but we are ready to GO!

Day 17: Tuesday, June 7th

You ever walk into a room where you can cut the tension with a knife?

That's what happened when I arrived the next day. I got to the hospital earlier this time. I wanted to be able to go down with Layla before the surgery just like the day before. As soon as I saw Jeremiah, I knew something was up. He had a look on his face that I couldn't read.

"She may not be getting the surgery today," he said quickly.

Advocating for your children is difficult. It was especially difficult in this case because we had to trust the doctors. It had to be a balance. Today's surgeon was willing to work on a pediatric but wanted to go in through Layla's mouth instead of her stomach. This wouldn't be an issue if Layla's jaw wasn't wired shut. So, to do surgery this way, they would need to remove the wires, perform the stomach surgery, and rewire her jaw. This was a hard stop. It seemed cruel to put her through that again, especially when there was another way.

Before I arrived, Jeremiah and the surgeon were discussing it. Both were standing firm on their decisions, so the conversation ended with us looking for another surgeon. Our arrival at Shepherd Center would be pushed back yet another day.

I have been praying for my kids since the day they were born. I pray for their future spouses, I pray for their safety and protection, I pray that they would have happy, full lives. With Layla, I would always pray we'd find a way to harness that boldness and it would be used for good. I knew very early on this chick had potential to change the world. This situation is not what I had in mind, but it's really serving that purpose. Since she has a bit of an audience now, we have together witnessed miracle after miracle. I haven't yet described the prognosis from the doctors in the beginning because it's physically painful to even think about, but I will say doctors have been really quiet lately. We are witnessing God at work through Layla. Giving people hope, putting everyday stresses into a different perspective, and realizing we really are not in control. In an instant your whole world can change, and there is no amount of money or connections that can fix it. But the love around you definitely helps. Her surgery was again rescheduled, and they are "potentially" doing it tomorrow. This will delay us leaving, but I guess that's good because I haven't started packing yet. She had a very sleepy day. She's still tracking with her eyes and lifting her arms a bit more than before, and I just thought this was cutest ever.

Day 18: Wednesday June 8th

Today was a good day to make friends.

Jeremiah and the surgeon from the prior day decided to put their disagreement behind them and do the surgery the way we wanted it. She was, once again, prepped for surgery and very active with the medications being withheld. Her left leg started doing some moving, and she could now bend her knee on command.

The stomach surgery was going to take a bit.
The air ambulance was taken care of.
We somewhat had a plan for our exit to Shepherd.
Now, my mind had time to wander.

We still had little details about the accident. We weren't even concerned about the how's or why's at that point. Dealing with the aftermath was our priority. Several people had reached out to me with information in the beginning, but I didn't want to know it then. I was only concerned with my daughter living. Now that things were more stable, I started to think more about it. I remembered someone telling me about a man they said helped Layla on scene. Maybe he's the one who called 911; I wasn't sure. I scrolled through my phone, and there it was: One of my many unanswered texts from the early days of this whole thing. The man's name was Oren, and he was another one of those "coincidences" sent our way. From the very beginning of this, Layla was in good hands, including Oren's.

It was time for me to thank this man and hear what happened that day. I sent a text asking for more information, and his reply filled in more gaps than I expected. He wrote:

Hi Ali, thank you for reaching out. I was waiting and hoping to hear from you. There is no way that I can comprehend what you have been going through. Just know that Layla and your family have been in my thoughts constantly. I am not religious in any way, but since that day, I have traveled to Israel. I asked a priest to pray for Layla by name at the Church of the Holy Sepulchre, one of the holiest Christian churches, and asked a rabbi to pray at the Wailing Wall, both in Jerusalem. Every little bit could help.

Just a quick background... My wife and I live about 15 or so houses down from the location of the crash. We have 2 boys, 14 and 5, and she is 6 months pregnant with a little girl. I am a former Army combat medic. After my service, I worked in New York City as a civilian paramedic while attending flight training. I am now a private jet pilot.

On that Sunday, I was with my 5-year-old all day while my wife was at work. She is an ICU nurse at JFK Hospital. My son and I went to the supermarket. As we drove back into the neighborhood, I decided to take the longer of the two ways to our home. We weren't in a rush. We stopped at a neighbor's house and got out of the car to say hi since he was outside. While we were saying goodbye, we saw the two girls driving by on the ATV. They were talking and giggling. This image will be imprinted in me forever. We got back in the car and continued to drive toward our house.

Moving forward, I will describe to you exactly what I saw and did. I will detail it enough so you can paint a picture of my view. I apologize in advance if this adds to your pain.

As we turned a bend in the street, I saw the ATV. It was stopped against the back of a parked red SUV. One girl was laying on the ground, the other was slumped over the handle bars. Both appeared to not be moving. I pulled my car in front of the SUV in an effort to block the view from my son.

As I exited my car, I could see two neighbors that came out of their homes, each on either side of the street. I told one gentleman that I am a paramedic and asked him if he could keep an eye on my son. I left the car running and quickly approached the girls.

The girl on the ground was regaining consciousness. The girl on the ATV initially did not appear to be breathing. After a closer assessment, I observed a breath about every 15-20 seconds. I turned off the ATV's engine and positioned myself on the right side of it. I supported her by cradling her lower jaw to keep it open with my right hand, and I used my left hand to slightly lift her by the waist of the back of her pants. I was trying to relieve the pressure she had on her chest and diaphragm caused by her body weight. It seemed to work, and her respirations improved. Her weight was shifted more to her armpits, and she was facing the ground at a 45 degree angle. I decided to hold position there, unless she stopped breathing, until EMS or someone else medically trained would arrive to assist. I could not see the front of her body from where I was standing. There was extensive damage to the ATV, and I was concerned about moving her. I was concerned that she had other injuries that I could not see.

While standing there, I had a neighbor call 911 and put them on speaker for me. I identified myself and gave them a quick description of what they needed to know. I suggested they send all resources, including dispatching the trauma hawk helicopter.

That same neighbor then asked my permission and took my son into her house.

85

I was then able to somewhat communicate with the girl on the ground. I was able to determine her name and that I was holding onto Layla. I could not get the last names but eventually got her address from her. I asked another neighbor/onlooker to go to that address and tell them that the girls on the ATV were involved in a crash. They arrived along with a large police, fire-rescue, and EMS response. The paramedics took over care, and I stepped aside once I gave them a verbal handover report.

The police took my statement, then instructed me to stay within the taped area and not to leave it. I had to wait for the vehicle homicide detectives since Layla was critically injured, and, although I did not actually witness the crash, I moved things and therefore disrupted the scene.

Other than for minor things, I have not treated a pediatric patient since 2006, prior to becoming a father. This has been challenging me daily. Layla is with me all day, every day since. Although nothing like Layla's pain or yours, it has certainly affected me. I hesitate each time I go on, but I have been reading every word you post in the Facebook group. Your strength is beyond remarkable.

Sending lots of love and prayers.

This was a lot to process. It rattled me but also brought comfort to know this man was with her. He seemed genuine and kind. He didn't have to stop that day; he could have continued home and enjoyed his Sunday. How many times had I driven by an accident without the thought of stopping ever occurring to me? I obviously didn't have the skill set this man had. He kept our daughter breathing until paramedics arrived. How can you ever repay something like that? I felt like a "thank you" would be silly in comparison to the gift he gave me. He was now connected to Layla and our family.

Something told me we were going to be friends after this.

Day 19: Thursday, June 9th

Tomorrow was the day we had been waiting for; we were finally leaving for Shepherd Center. We were just waiting for some sort of insurance paperwork to come over. I had to pack up her hospital room, then head home to finish packing Cali and myself. It was difficult packing for an indefinite amount of time, and I didn't want to bring too much clutter.

Jeremiah and I decided he would ride with Layla. I was willing to go, but he felt I would be more of a distraction if I did. I have a fear of flying—a bad one. He was right; we didn't want to risk a panic attack up there! Jenna was going to drive me and Cali up in my car before flying back home. I was willing to drive myself, but I was very distracted with admission to Shepherd, so it probably wasn't safe. Jenna, being the friend she is, offered to help. I think this was hard for her, too. We had always been inseparable—a package deal. We did everything together. It was common that we even ran errands together. This felt like the last errand we would run for a while. We would no longer be seven houses away from each other. The idea of this wrecked me. Whenever I broke down about it, Jenna would promise I could do it and assure me she'd be up to visit as much as possible.

After I said my goodbyes to the hospital staff, I headed home to pack. I had mentioned to Kathleen that day how much Layla would hate her dirty hair. That girl always had freshly washed hair! The best I could manage was the dry shampoo and detangler. After I arrived home, Jeremiah sent some pictures of Kathleen giving Layla a proper hair wash before her exit the next day. That simple act felt so significant to me. She was finally getting all the dirt and blood rinsed off her from that awful day. It was one step closer to putting that accident further behind us. Nurses don't typically wash the patient's hair, not like this. Kathleen wasn't even our nurse. She worked in step down care, I believe as some sort of manager. This job seemed way below her pay grade, and she was already off the clock. She was sending my girl off with a clean head of hair for no other reason than to be kind. It was her final act of kindness to us at St. Mary's, but my friendship with Kathleen was just beginning. For that and all the other things she did for us while we were there, I will be forever grateful.

Once Kathleen was finished with her work, she passed the job of styling to Naomi. Naomi is Jeremiah's sister who is also a nurse. She was there for her last visit before we headed to Georgia. We love Naomi in our family! She is sweet, and gentle, and always took the job of being an aunt very seriously. Every Christmas, she would buy the kids an experience. With it, she gave them an invaluable gift: her time. She would tailor these experiences around each kid, so they each went separately. Layla always picked those painting places; it had become their thing. When Naomi got married to Joel, he knew he signed up for uncle duties in the same way. They were always in attendance for the many sports my kids played and often joined us for Sunday dinners. In short, they were winning the aunt and uncle game in every way.

They had the potential to be the most amazing parents; everyone saw that. What everyone didn't know was they were struggling to get pregnant. Often, I wondered how that was fair. These were two perfect people who wanted the role of parents. Two people who would be so good at it. How could it possibly be fair that they may never get it? During one of our heart-to-heart conversations about it, Naomi told me she had peace about it. She said if God wanted her to be a mom, she would be. If they were only going to be aunt and uncle, if that's what

God wanted, they were okay with that, too. This is what faith and obedience look like to me, even if it didn't seem fair.

Naomi was actually pregnant at the time of Layla's accident, but she had not released that news to the world yet. I worried about that a lot—that this situation would be too much for her body and her pregnancy in its early stages. She had miscarried not long before this pregnancy, and it was devastating. I wanted to put her in a bubble to protect her from this, but it wouldn't have mattered. Nothing was going to stop her from seeing Layla. That day, she braided Layla's hair, prayed over her, and said a painful goodbye to her brother and niece.

We were still waiting for that insurance paperwork to come over. It was some sort of authorization holding us up. In these situations, insurance works week to week. They don't want to pay for any more time than they deem you need. Our doctors would have to submit weekly notes until insurance felt she was well enough to send us home. The insurance had only sent over a three-day authorization, and we were leaving on a Friday. That meant, come Monday, we would be free loading at Shepherd. That's why the Center asked for a seven-day authorization in order for us to leave. We had until 5:00 that day for the correction to be made; otherwise, we were going to have to wait until Monday. The air ambulance was waiting on our confirmation, too, and there was a possibility they could be booked if we didn't get back to them in time.

With half an hour left, we still knew nothing.

Jeremiah: Nothing?

Me: Nada.

Jeremiah: Even if we get the form, the next problem will be if there is a flight for tomorrow available. Last I heard, there were only two left and that was at 2 PM. Make sure you answer every phone call.

Me: Will do. I still have faith.

Jeremiah: The suspense is killing me.

Me: Me too.

Moments later, the case manager rushed into the room to tell Jeremiah she received the paperwork. We had clearance to go with minutes to spare. The flight was secured, and tomorrow, we would leave for our new home.

Me: Flight team is going to call you with itinerary.

Jeremiah: 10 AM leave St. Mary's
11:35 depart Palm Beach
1:20 land in Forsyth County airport
2:30 arrive at Shepherd

Me: It's happening, babe.

Jeremiah: What time are you leaving?

Me: Aiming for 5:30 AM, should beat you there. Text me tomorrow. I love you so much. Next adventure begins.

Jeremiah: Yep! Turn the page!

THE SHEPHERD CENTER

Day 20: Friday, June 10th

Jenna is not a morning person, but she got up at the crack of dawn for me. I was hoping to beat Layla's flight by enough time that I could get Cali settled into Bethany's house before meeting Layla at Shepherd. Bethany is Mary Jane's oldest daughter. She and her husband, Jonathan, had offered their basement to us. We would use that as our home base while figuring things out in Georgia. It was a kind thing to do. They had two small children of their own and were probably looking forward to a peaceful summer. Housing us held a lot of uncertainties. We weren't sure what our schedule would look like or how much help we were going to need with Cali. They gladly signed up for it all and assured me everything would work out.

Jenna, Cali, and I hit the road on schedule and watched the sunrise about an hour into our drive. Layla loved to go watch the sunrise on the beach. It was one of her favorite things to do. The last sunrise I saw with her was the day of her birthday party the year before. She convinced me to let a group of girls spend the night. The plan was to grab Starbucks in the morning and go watch the sunrise. The issue was she was going to pull an all-nighter to make that happen, and I needed sleep. They kept me up most of the night, even after my threats of cancelling the beach trip failed to keep them quiet. In the morning, I caved and took them anyway. Sometimes you have to pick your battles as a parent, and now, I'm so glad I didn't fight that one. If I had, we wouldn't have seen that

93

last sunrise together. And now, unsure we'd get to see another one together, I was so glad I had that memory.

These kinds of memories were constantly coming to mind for Jeremiah and me. We'd think on the things we'd done and seen with our girl. We'd pick out the parts we wished we'd done differently. All the moments we didn't realize might have been the last. Each time we had this conversation, we'd come to the same conclusion: We were unable to change the past, but this would impact how we appreciated our future.

Jeremiah was constantly sending me updates on Layla. He had strict instructions to send me play-by-play pictures. The medical transportation team had arrived and loaded her onto the stretcher. The entire ICU staff had lined up along the walls to say goodbye as they paraded her out of the unit. Someone had attached balloons to her stretcher and got her a new blanket (a pink one of course). They tearfully sent her off and made us promise to come back as visitors next time. Obviously, it was an emotional exit.

They rode by ambulance to Palm Beach airport. She was tucked into the stretcher as if in a little cocoon. She was on minimal medications at this point; she only needed a few at night. She had an IV for fluids, and her trach was capped. Her vitals were being monitored by a mobile unit now, and there was a team with her in case anything went wrong. Her expression was one of indifference. She clearly had no idea what was happening. The ambulance drove right on the runway directly to her private jet. Door to door service practically! They loaded her up in the jet and tucked her into a secure area. She had grown attached to the stress ball from Cali and held on to it during the whole thing.

Just before they took off, Jeremiah sent me one final picture of Layla in the jet ready to go.

Me: It's surreal. Pray with her. I love you both so much. I'm crying, and I don't know why. I can't believe we got here. Thank you for being you.

Jeremiah: Thank YOU for being you. I wouldn't want to do this with anyone else. We are taking off. See you there.

The closer we got to Georgia, the more anxious I got. My reality hit me in two waves, first when I saw the "Thank you for visiting Florida" sign and again when I saw the "Welcome to Georgia" sign. I couldn't believe we were doing this. We just moved to Georgia. We just left our family and friends behind. We just left our home with our dogs. I had been so focused on *why* we were doing it, I hadn't really processed the reality of actually doing it.

That's when I started to panic.

I love my home. It means something very sentimental to me. My parents divorced when I was young, and eventually, my mom sold our house and moved us in with her sister. My aunt and uncle are amazing people who love me like their own, but their home wasn't my home. So, one of the first things I wanted as an adult was a home of my own. A place no one could take from me. A place I could ensure only good memories remained. When our friends were buying fun things with their money, we were saving for that home. It was a dream that became reality for us, and now, that home was our safe place. Our children all grew up there. I couldn't imagine not waking up there every day. I was starting to spiral, but I had to focus on the road ahead, not the one behind. I had to remember why we were doing this. It wouldn't be forever. Besides, home was wherever we were, and for a while, that was going to be Georgia.

We were still an hour away when we hit Atlanta traffic. Jeremiah was already en route from the airport to Shepherd, and it looked like he was going to beat us there. There wouldn't be time to get Cali settled at Bethany's before going myself, so Jenna was going to do that after dropping me at Shepherd.

When we finally pulled into the parking lot, the first thing I saw was a massive bronze statue of a man in a wheelchair holding a javelin. I imagined maybe this was the founder or, at the very least, something with a good story behind it. There was a sign outside the entrance that gave me hope. It read:

Through these doors, wonderful things will happen.

I really hoped it was right.

I made my way up to security and let them know where I was headed. The man at the desk directed me where to go from there. When I stepped out of the elevator, I saw a nurse's station to my right. They instructed me to take another right, and I would run into her door at the end of the hallway. In the ICU, one of the walls was glass, so you could see into all the rooms like fishbowls. Jeremiah was always closing the curtain in front of it for privacy, but I never thought about how safe that glass made me feel until now. The nurses could see into her room if there was an emergency. In this place, there were no glass walls. These were more like regular hospital rooms, only a little bigger.

As I was heading down the hall, I saw a few of the patients out and about. Most of these patients were adults, the majority being male adults. I wondered where all the kids were. Did they put Layla in an adult wing by mistake? I reached her door to see her name sketched on the name plate outside: "L. Rogan." This was officially her room.

When I opened the door, I immediately noticed the lack of equipment. Where were all her machines? I knew at the very least she needed the thing that monitored her heart and blood pressure. Layla was in bed with Jeremiah sitting at her side. Her eyes were closed, and there were different colored wires coming out from the new hospital gown she wore. Her trach was now capped with what looked like a green sponge. Her feeding tube pole was close by, and there was a cart next to her bed with some sort of gadget. I later found out that gadget was a respiratory device used in her breathing treatments. The wires were connected to a small grey box in the bed. This little box was monitoring her vitals. If something was to go wrong, it would alert the nurse's station to come check it out.

My first thought? I didn't like it.
My second thought? This isn't safe.

How could she graduate to so much independence in a day? I started to think that maybe we made a bad choice. Maybe she wasn't ready for this yet.

There was staff coming and going, getting her settled and adjusted. We were meeting so many new faces that it was hard to remember who did what. All of a sudden, a nurse appeared with bright pink hair. This made me smile. If Layla could talk, she would tell her, "Pink is my favorite color!" Our pink-haired nurse introduced herself as Laura, and we liked her instantly. During our introduction, I started expressing my concerns with her. Laura tried assuring me that Layla would be safe and cared for here, but still, I broke down. I was scared. I wanted to go back to the ICU where I was comfortable. I wanted her machines back. I wanted a pediatric unit with kids, not all these adults. I wanted her room close to the nurse's station, not the furthest from them. Laura was calm and gentle with me. She understood my shock; I'm sure she'd seen it before. Eventually, she went to grab the charge nurse, Kenneth, to give me more peace about Layla's arrival to Shepherd.

We instantly liked Kenneth, too. He told us that Shepherd did not have a pediatric unit because they did not take pediatric patients. In order to get in, patients had to weigh 100 pounds and have gone through puberty. He assured me the box watching her vitals was heavily monitored. Finally, he asked if I wanted a camera installed in her room for 24/7 surveillance. These cameras were typically used for unruly patients that needed to be watched constantly, not for someone like Layla. Still, he offered it to give me peace of mind.

"You'll see in a couple days what we are all about," he told me. "She is safe here, and it's going to be okay."

97

I wanted to believe him so badly, but I felt unsettled still. The original plan was to eventually leave Layla at night and go home to Cali, but there was no way I could leave her here alone yet. I wanted to revise the plan, so I asked Jeremiah if he could manage to stay a little longer. Of course, he agreed.

With that settled, I got to work acclimating to our new living space. There was a little chair that converted to a bed, just like at St. Mary's ICU. There were tons of closets and shelves, and we now had our own bathroom. She had two windows in her room, and one overlooked Peachtree Street. I set up her diffuser and made a little station for some of her things. I wanted to find a way to make this place feel cozy. They gave me free reign to decorate and make ourselves as comfortable as we needed. So, I was going to do just that!

Jenna returned to pick me up and take me back to Bethany's. It was a 30-minute drive for me to unload all my fears. Jenna usually knows what to say, but this was unchartered territory. It's hard for anyone to relate to any of this. She just kept encouraging me to give it time. As we pulled into the driveway, I agreed to try.

As I was rambling on, Jenna paused. In the yard was one of those big signs you usually see for graduations or birthdays. In big pink and silver letters, it read "Layla Strong." Then, I noticed the pink ribbons trailing down the street on the neighbors' mailboxes. I was speechless. Like mouth open, frozen. Did they really do this for us? My cousin? Her entire neighborhood? It took me a minute to process the kindness behind it all. To this day, I am still in awe.

I headed in to thank my new roommates for the warm welcome. Cali was excited to show me around the basement. This was more like a little apartment. It had a bedroom, bathroom, living room area, and a small kitchen. Bethany had stocked the kitchen with all my favorite things. She obviously had help because my tastes are very specific. She had lemons for my water and my favorite protein powders, amongst various snacks both Cali and I enjoy. She even had a diffuser and oils set up in the bedroom. Once again, I was hit with how kind these gestures were. I was choking back tears, really trying not to cry on my first day. These were happy tears though. I was just so touched by the way they welcomed us. They had done everything they could to make this feel like home, and right now, home meant a lot to me.

There was a door in the basement that led to the backyard. The backyard was Cali's favorite part. She had always been an outside kid, and this was like her own forest playground. There was a zip line, a trampoline, tons of paths and trails, and an actual playground. It gave me peace knowing how much she was going to enjoy this. Bethany's two little girls were excited to have their older cousin to play with, too. All three girls headed outside almost immediately after we settled in. Bethany and Jonathan are easy to be around, so conversation came easy. I joked we were now roomies, a nickname that would stick.

Finally, I started to relax. Things were good here. It was reassuring, and it made up for the unease I felt about Shepherd. It was one less thing to worry about. Jenna was supposed to fly out that night, but I convinced her to stay with me one more day. I was delaying the inevitable; I didn't want to say goodbye. She knew this and obliged me by spending one more night—my first night in my little apartment.

Well, we are here. Another step along the way. Me and Cali are staying with family about 30 minutes from the hospital. The neighbors all put pink bows on their mailboxes, and we were received with open arms. Cali loves playing outside and has been enjoying all the room to run. Shepherd Center is an amazing, beautiful place but very different than before. It's overwhelming. I was used to the ICU and oddly comfortable there. I will just need to learn to make this home. Here, Layla is independent of the tons of machines we were used to looking at. I don't doubt she is safe, but safe looks very different here, and it's taking me a minute to adjust to it. The weekends are a little calmer here. They have every patient on a very structured schedule (I love schedules) and the real stuff will begin Monday. It's an adjustment for all of us I suppose. Still not sure how our routine will work yet. Monday, I will meet her team and have a better idea. Keep praying please. This was a huge victory just getting her here, but there's a lot to be done, including adjusting me and Cali to a new place.

Day 21: Saturday, June 11th

Jenna booked a flight for the next morning, and Bethany offered to drive her to the airport. I was going to attempt my first run to Shepherd solo. Bethany programmed my navigation to get me there and, with the touch of another button, to get me home. Jenna understood my disability with directions better than anyone, so she knew this drive would be a big milestone for me. It was one thing getting lost at home; this was another state and the city of Atlanta on top of it. Bethany offered to drive in front of me, but eventually, I was going to have to learn this on my own. I figured it might as well be now.

There was something empowering about that drive. This was not something I typically would have attempted. I was navigating my way to the hospital, and the traffic wasn't intimidating me. I was so focused on reaching my girl that my usual fears were silent. I could do this; I *would* do this.

When I reached Layla, the first thing I noticed was they had dressed her. We had become so accustomed to the hospital gown, so it was refreshing to see her in regular clothes. These weren't her clothes, because Jeremiah was waiting for me to arrive with her suitcase I had packed. I left it at Bethany's the day before because we didn't expect they would be dressing her so soon. Now, there she was, wearing an oversized red t-shirt and sweatpants. She looked comfortable, almost like a normal teenager just lounging in the bed. Except she wasn't sitting still.

Her left leg was repeatedly picking up the blanket with her toes and dropping it. It was a restless type of movement, and it was odd seeing her move so much. I approached the bed and asked for her hand. She surprised me when she slowly gave it to me.

The day before they had fitted her for her wheelchair. I wasn't there to witness how it went down, but I knew it disturbed Jeremiah, so I didn't ask much about it. Today, I was going to find out why. To get Layla into it, she had to be picked up out of bed with a hydraulic lift. There was a lift sheet that was fit under her body before it was attached to the lift. With the touch of a button, it raised her into the air like a sack of potatoes. Then, they could navigate her body where they wanted to put her. They moved her until she was hovering over the wheelchair, then slowly brought her down. Once she was in the chair, she was strapped in across her chest so she wouldn't fall out. There was a head rest with pieces that came out like a halo to prevent her head from falling over. It was intense. How were we going to do this on our own?

Layla came to Shepherd with a bed sore, which was common in her condition. Originally, St. Mary's thought it was a birthmark, but over time, it escalated into somewhat of a problem. It had to be treated constantly, and she had to be turned frequently. Because of it, we couldn't leave her sitting upright in the wheelchair for more than twenty minutes. The nurse handed us a timer and showed us how to recline her chair back. We would have to take turns reclining and sitting her upright every twenty minutes. I was trying to focus on the fact she was out of bed, but it was difficult. It was so overwhelming to me. I started thinking about the people I knew who were confined to wheelchairs and wondered if this was what life was like for them. I wondered if this would be Layla's future. Would she be okay with that?

Eventually, the nurse came back and helped get her back into her bed. Weekends at Shepherd ran a little differently. There was a smaller staff, and the halls weren't as busy. Jeremiah and I learned how to get food delivered there for us, but we had to take a ten-minute walk to get it from the security guard. This worked fine with the two of us, but how would we manage this if we were alone? It's not that we couldn't leave Layla. Other than her kicking everything off the bed, she didn't do a lot of moving. We just didn't want to leave her, even for ten minutes. We saw many patients there alone, and it seemed sad to me. Where were their people? We were repeatedly told that no one remembers this stage, but we didn't care. We wanted to be there for every moment; even if she didn't remember, we would. The nursing staff came in about every two hours, but we couldn't bear the thought of her sitting in a quiet room alone for two hours. To us, she was still Layla. We had to have hope that she was somewhere inside there. Being left alone would have scared her if she was, so for now, we could manage taking shifts watching over her. That would be the plan.

As we familiarized ourselves with the place and the staff, we started to relax a little. I wasn't ready to get rid of the surveillance camera Kenneth had put in her room for us yet, but I was heading in the right direction. I was getting comfortable with this new reality.

Now, I needed to figure out my return to work. My plan was to work remotely from the hospital, so we set up my laptop and did a few test runs. Come Monday, Layla would have therapy several hours a day, so I thought I would work during that time. My company had been supportive during all of this and managed my business in my absence, but I felt guilty about it. It was silly, I know. They never made me feel like it was a problem, and they seemed more than willing to help me as long as I needed. This guilt was a "me" thing. I think a part of me just wanted the distraction—something that felt like my life before.

I situated Jeremiah with his dinner, then headed home to Cali. It was our first day of what I thought would be our schedule for a while, and it didn't seem so bad. I was doing surprisingly well navigating the city. I picked up Cali and headed to a grocery store to grab some dinner. Then, we had some photos printed for Layla's room. I had mixed feelings about putting up those pictures. I wanted to remind her of who she was, but I also didn't want to make her sad if that wasn't who she was anymore. Cali and I also bought markers and a poster-board for a project. We were going to make an "About Me" board for Layla's room. We thought it would be a good way for the nurses and therapists to know who she was and what she liked—a conversation starter, even if it was one sided. It was also a way to involve Cali in Layla's care. We finished up and tucked ourselves in for the night, celebrating another day completed.

So today we were on our own. Cali had a fun day planned with cousins, and I drove myself to and from the hospital. I even hit a grocery store. If you know me, you know this is a big deal. We got to meet some more of the staff, I only broke down to 2 of them, I only got lost once, and we figured out food delivery to the center. I'd say it was a successful day with minimal bumps. I love that they don't wear hospital gowns here, and it was nice seeing Layla in real clothes. She got to do some minimal PT and start adjusting to her new place. She's tracking a lot more with eyes now. It's so cool. And she's moving her left side a lot. She kicks pillows and blankets off the bed constantly, and we've never been so happy to pick up her stuff. Almost looks like she's doing cheerleading. She's following commands better each day, and my personal favorite is giving me her hand. She misses sometimes, but she's listening, so for now that's good enough for me. Fun fact... the place is full. Layla got one of the last beds. Even one of the nurses explained how hard it is to get in. Just another example of God's hand in this and knowing we are in the right place.

Day 22: Sunday, June 12th

It was our 18th wedding anniversary.

I guess nothing says, "for better or worse," like spending an anniversary in a hospital.

Trauma can have a significant impact on a marriage. I knew the statistics related to traumatic events and divorce. After trauma, you go into a sort of survival mode. Sometimes, you withdraw from the world, and that can include your spouse. It can really destroy a marriage. I was well versed in this because I spent a lot of time in therapy after my brother died. That was just an appetizer compared to this. From the beginning, this worried me. Would our marriage sustain this? Would we turn on each other? Would we isolate from each other? The only thing I was completely sure of was neither of us would hurt our kids. We would do anything for those kids. Our marriage wasn't always pretty, but it was always special. We had beat the odds. We started out with nothing and overcame a lot of things to arrive where we were today. It seemed like a waste to throw it all away now. The better solution seemed to be uniting in this trauma. In ways, we became bonded by the pain. We gave each other space to grieve and heal in our unique ways, and we respected that space. If I'm being honest, we almost seemed to get along better than before the accident. We were taking on this giant together. My weakness was his strength and vice versa. Our differences had always balanced well, and it was the same in our grief.

We usually went to dinner for our anniversary, and I loved those dinners. I was a more adventurous eater than Jeremiah, but he was always a good sport about it. Over the last 18 years, I had learned to cook and gotten pretty good at it. Cooking was a stress reliever for me. I loved cooking. I put a lot of love in my meals, and seeing others enjoy them was my favorite part. It wasn't always that way. The first thing I ever made for Jeremiah was Hamburger Helper. I was 22, and I remember walking through the grocery store trying to conjure up something I could cook for my new man. I stumbled on the box of Hamburger Helper and thought it seemed easy enough. I was so proud of that boxed meal. He graciously ate the entire thing and sang my praises. Since it was the only thing I knew how to make, I made it every day for quite a while. Finally, he politely suggested maybe I should give something else a try. We still laugh about that. Thankfully for both of us, my cooking leveled up quite a bit from my Hamburger Helper days.

This year there would be no fancy dinner or home-cooked meal. So, we would bring our anniversary dinner to Shepherd Center. We selected a restaurant a little more upscale than our normal hospital meals and had it delivered. We even ordered appetizers to make it feel different than our usual Door Dash dates. I set up Layla's tray table between us to create our own little dining space. I set the table with the disposable silverware and plates I found in the hospital family break room, and we dined at Layla's bedside. Just like our date at St. Mary's, I found the whole situation comical, so much so that I giggled through our meal. Then I snapped a picture of us. I wanted to remember this moment forever.

We finished our meal, and I started decorating her room. I was hanging up the pictures I printed as well as a few cards I brought from Florida and a poster board her cheer team made. My goal was to wallpaper that room with love and encouragement. Above her bed, Jeremiah was hanging a tapestry that read, "For this child, I have prayed." This was a special decoration because Mary Jane's daughter, Jessica, had given it to us. People often thought Jessica and I were sisters. It was such a compliment to me whenever people said that. Jessica is beautiful inside and out—easily one of my favorite people. She had her mom bring down the tapestry during their trip to Florida. I got chills when Mary Jane first handed it to me because I knew the value of this tapestry to Jessica and her family. She and her husband, Mack, struggled to get pregnant. They were another couple I knew would make perfect parents. They were always so good to my own children, and my kids adored them. After a few, cruel years trying to have a baby the natural way, they were blessed with Charlie, a beautiful little girl they adopted. This was Charlie's tapestry—the one that hung in her room. The tapestry represented their reward after faithfully waiting and praying for their girl.

And it's exactly what we were doing for Layla now.

I loved the way the decorations seemed to light up the room. They made it feel less like a hospital and more like a bedroom. Layla loved redecorating her room at home, and she was always up to date on the latest trends. This was the first time since her baby nursery I was allowed to have a say in the décor. I didn't have a say in much with Layla when the teenage years hit. Suddenly, I became uncool and, according to her, "the strictest parents out of all her friends." I hated how we'd grown apart, but my job was to be her mom first. I always thought we'd have time to be friends later.

Layla was growing increasingly more active. Her left leg and arm never seemed to sit still; it almost seemed like she couldn't control it. She was mindlessly grabbing things like the blanket or her ball and setting them back down. She would pick at her bandages, blankets, and clothes. To say she was restless would be an understatement. The concern was she'd grab her trach or stomach PEG and pull them out. That meant it was time for those restraints again. They were identical to the ones at St. Mary's—a thick padded bracelet that wrapped around her wrist with Velcro and attached to a nylon strap secured to the bed. We could adjust the length and give her more freedom, but we rarely did this at first. She grabbed anything she could reach, and the stomach peg was dangerously close. She could also reach the bandages on her left leg that covered the third-degree burns she had on her thighs from the accident. These were gruesome. They were gasoline burns that had to be treated frequently by a wound care team. It was important we kept the area untouched and clean, and of course, she loved picking at them. We were allowed to remove the restraints if we were closely watching her. When we did, we had to physically hold her hand to keep it still. She seemed to enjoy having her palm scratched, so we did that often in holding her hand. She would even scratch ours back, but I think she was only doing it to show us what she wanted.

I would be spending the night with her that night. Tomorrow was the first day of her regular therapy, and I would need to familiarize myself with our new routine before Jeremiah headed back to Florida. Jeremiah had pushed our sleeping chair up against Layla's bed so he could hold her hand until she fell asleep. I thought it was sweet, so I left it there and prepared for my first night at Shepherd.

Sundays at Shepherd are "rest days." Someone should have told Layla that because she'd done anything but rest. But that's a good thing! She even earned herself some restraints after figuring out how to escape the mitts. She only needs to wear the restraints if she isn't being supervised, which between me and Dad, is basically never. She just feels more like Layla each day. I think we spent an hour scratching each other's hands today, and honestly, it was just so peaceful and special. I keep thinking of our life pre-accident, and between all of our schedules, we were always pretty busy and sometimes forgot to take time to enjoy quiet moments like this. So... lesson learned. She's already winning over the nurses, and we've enjoyed getting to know them. I started decorating the room today and learned I can go crazy with it. We are filling the walls with pictures and cards she received. Starting to feel more comfortable here. Tomorrow is a big day. We start her regular schedule, and this girl is busy! I'm excited to meet her team and watch them work their magic. Layla has always been very coachable and willing to put in the extra work. I expect this won't be any different.

108

Day 23: Monday, June 13th

It was easier to sleep at Shepherd Center than St. Mary's. It was definitely quieter here. Regardless, I was so anxious for the next day that I tossed and turned until our door popped open at 6:30 am. Standing in my doorway was a very animated blond girl who quickly bounced into our room and introduced herself as Corrie. It was so nice to meet this part of our support system face to face. She seemed so comfortable in this environment, hopping right up on Layla's bed. She was reviewing our schedule and examining Layla like she'd seen this hundreds of times. She translated the schedule for me and said Layla would be getting a shower that morning followed by a few additional therapies. Then, she told me where I could get a cup of coffee and promised to check on me later. Even though it was the first time we were meeting in person, Corrie felt like an old friend, and it was comforting to have a friend there.

For the life of me, I couldn't picture how they were going to manage getting Layla in a shower. Showering fell under the category of occupational therapy for now. Eventually, they would train me to do it, but I was far from ready. Shepherd had training for everything. If we wanted to learn something, they would teach us so we could be signed off to do it independently. The goal was to give anyone the tools they'd need to care for their person when they went home. The challenge was they weren't sure what skills we'd need because things changed day to day. We were dying to care for Layla more ourselves. There was something special about taking care of her. She may have been 15, but she was still our baby, and right now, she needed us for everything.

Emily was Layla's occupational therapist. She was soft spoken and gentle. Right away, I knew Layla would like her. Even though Layla was oblivious, I was grateful it was Emily that would be showering her. Layla was modest when it came to undressing, even in front of me. Emily had a calm voice and explained the process to me step by step. We used the bed lift to transfer Layla into a new wheelchair. This one was made for the shower so it was able to get wet. The only thing that couldn't get wet was her trach. If water got inside, she could asphyxiate. I didn't realize that was how that worked and immediately started doubting my ability to do it on my own. Counting me, it would take three of us to shower her that first time. Emily's helper basically held a towel around Layla's neck the entire time to keep her trach dry. Emily did the majority of the work, but I was at her side, following any instructions she gave me. The entire time she narrated everything and explained why she was doing it.

That shower was emotional for me but not necessarily in a bad way. There was an aspect of it that was sad, but I was also so grateful to be able to help do this for my daughter. I was learning to bathe her, just like I did when she was a baby. I already felt bonded to Emily because of this. It was like she was giving me a gift by teaching me how to care for Layla in this way. It took about 40 minutes from start to finish, mostly because I slowed them down. Emily encouraged me, promising it would get easier. I didn't fully believe her yet, but I already knew I trusted her.

The next member of Layla's therapy team I would meet was Jen, the speech therapist. She arrived at our room and told us we would be heading to the gym for her session. Jen had a good demeanor. She came across as very intelligent, and I could tell she would push Layla. I liked that about her. Layla could be tough, so she was going to need someone tougher to get her to try. Speech therapy was an important part of this process. Jen was not only responsible for Layla learning to speak again, she would also be helping her with cognition, breathing, swallowing, and eating. These things seemed impossible to us at that time, but Jen didn't seem intimidated by any of it. Jen was also in a wheelchair. Something about that gave me hope. This woman had obviously overcome something pretty significant, and she was also clearly thriving. I was hopeful Layla could be like her one day. If nothing else, she could at least firsthand relate to some of this. Like with Emily, I trusted Jen immediately. So together, we loaded Layla up into her wheelchair and headed to the gym.

The gym was located on the other side of the elevators. I had seen it from afar but never looked inside for long. It was a strange surge of emotions stepping inside for the first time. The space was a lot larger than I expected. There was equipment everywhere and lots of small groups working throughout the room. I didn't mean to stare at the patients, but I couldn't help it. If we were lucky, Layla would progress to these stages. I knew what it would look like in theory, but it was a lot different seeing it in person. Any one of them could be Layla's future— a fact I wasn't ready to face yet. As much as it scared me, there was also a feeling of jealousy. These patients could also do things she couldn't. Just seeing the ones who could maneuver their wheelchairs made me envious. Still, there were all levels of disabilities here, and they all reminded me how difficult this was going to be. Jen led us toward the back where the therapy tables were, and she and her team began working with Layla.

That evening, as promised, Corrie checked on me.

Corrie: So, how has the first day been?

Me: Overwhelming, but great.

Corrie: How was her shower?

Me: She loved it.

Corrie: Did she use left hand to help at all?

Me: Oh yes. That was actually really funny to see. She washed her tummy and legs.

Corrie: Yes! She's a 4! They can't say it yet, but she is.

Me: Really!? How do you know?

Corrie: Because she's super restless and she waved goodbye to me. She helped wash and she's following commands and tracking. These are not things a 3 does. She needs to follow commands three days in a row to be considered out of a 3. But she's not a 3. A 3 is going to have their eyes open, but they may not track and may not respond to audible or visual startle. They may follow some commands, but it's not going to be consistent.

Me: Oh hallelujah! I needed a victory today.

Corrie: You've had a lot of victories today. Now, we wait and watch and see what 4 turns into. Is she going to stay restless? Is she going to get agitated? Will she be combative? I see it all as a victory.
Tomorrow, Jen will do the CRS test with her and Emily.

Me: What's CRS test?

Corrie: CRS is the coma recovery scale. It's what we use to monitor whether someone has emerged or not. She must follow commands with speech and OT together for three days in a row. The screening addresses functional object use, visual and auditory startle, simple command following, etc.

Me: Oh. I like it. I hope she's ready. We practice a lot.

Corrie: She is. She's ready.

Hearing Corrie say those words meant a lot to me. I had never experienced anything like this before, so I had no clue what progress looked like for her. Layla still seemed miles away from the daughter I remembered. I couldn't even picture an assessment of her because she didn't really do anything measurable, at least not to me. She had a few tricks—wiggling toes and fingers, waving hello, thumbs up—but she didn't really do anything without us asking. The only movements she made on her own seemed involuntary and tiresome, like her body was stuck in a loop. The look in her eyes was the most painful part. It's crazy how eyes can show the life inside. At a young age, Layla started getting migraines. I'm talking adult-strength migraines where she would end up vomiting all day. You could always tell it was coming by the look in her eyes. When the migraine would finally pass, life would return to those eyes again. Now, her eyes looked similar to one of those migraine days. Maybe these therapists had some magic trick to wake her up. Maybe this CRS thing would give us some answers.

I swear to you in that moment it was like Layla heard my thoughts. As I was leaving, she turned over on her side and wrapped her little arm around a pillow. *This* looked like Layla. It was a very normal thing for a teenage girl to do. She looked like I would find her in her room at home sleeping. Typically now, she laid flat on her back, and we had to use those wedges we stuck under her to turn her. This turn she made on her own. It was the most precious thing I'd ever seen. I had to soak it up awhile before leaving her to return home to Cali for the night. It was as if Layla was letting me know she was still in there, giving me the strength to get to the next day.

Today was very busy. She had physical therapy, occupational therapy, some psych thing, speech therapy, and she did some of this from a wheelchair vs. a bed. I figured out where the coffee was, and I got to see the therapy room, also filled with patients. Definitely was an eye opener, I'm still processing that. On the one hand, you just can't believe this is happening to you, but then you see how many people it's happening to. Each therapy and step today were difficult for me at first. Every step has the potential to be what her life looks like, and I had to process and accept that and trust we will be able to handle whatever this may be. But I do have faith. I have faith she's far from finished fighting. Day 1 is done. Brighter days are coming.

Day 24: Tuesday, June 14th

Cali's mood had been declining. The idea of moving to Georgia originally excited her. She loved it there. She loved the people there. But now, the reality was starting to become apparent: Her mom and dad would not be as present as she wanted. The one night I spent away from her had taken a toll, and Jeremiah urged me to switch. He stressed how much Cali needed her mom. She had always been attached to me more than anyone, so this was especially difficult for her. I could see this was going to become a tug of war between my daughters. How was I going to manage this when Jeremiah returned to Florida?

It was my day to take Cali's mind off the situation, and I needed to be creative. Jessica had mentioned a pet store where you could hold puppies. Today, puppies seemed like the perfect idea. After breakfast, we ventured to the store. I was expecting a few puppies at best, but this place had every breed you could fathom. They were all separated by glass windows and seemed to be paired by sizes. I gave Cali the task of picking the puppy we would play with that day. This was a very serious decision for her. She walked up to each section, slowly examining them all. She was checking for cuteness and temperament. Finally, she chose her guy. They put us in a little pen where the puppy could roam free. The giggles that came out of her were the most beautiful thing I had heard in a while, and I knew this was the perfect place for her. She had a smile plastered on her face while the puppy climbed all over her. She decided to name him Walter, even though he wasn't ours. I knew then that we would be returning to name other puppies during our stay.

We are a dog family. We've always had dogs around since the kids were little. Currently we had two chocolate labs at home, Kaia and Koa. We had gotten Kaia after a bet with Layla when she was nine. We were at the beach when Layla announced to her dad, "If I can break the world record for back handsprings, you have to take me to the shelter to get a dog!" It seemed like a bet we couldn't lose, so we agreed. The record was 30, but not in the sand. The sand was much harder. Layla gave it her best shot, getting up to 17 before she collapsed. Then, she would get back up and do it again. This continued until her ankles started giving out, and I instructed Jeremiah to call it off. Something told me we were going to either end up in a hospital or at the pound, possibly both.

We brought Kaia home the next morning.

Later that day, the cousins took over for me with Cali so I could return to Shepherd for the CRS test. We were told we wouldn't be allowed to come along for it, but Jen said if we remained quiet, she'd allow it. The scene looked similar to the day before. They strapped Layla into her wheelchair and took her to the therapy table in the back of the gym. They used the lift to get her transferred to the table. Emily was behind her supporting her back and head from falling over, and there was another therapist positioned in front for the same reason. Jen was on Layla's left side in front and would be administering the test. She held a hairbrush in one hand and a ball in the other and her hands were spread far apart. She started by asking Layla to look at the ball. Looking on, Jeremiah and I both chuckled. This was not something Layla was able to do.

Just like that, Layla's eyes shot up to Jen's right hand.

I looked at Jeremiah dumbfounded and found he had the same expression as me. Then Jen asked her to look at the hairbrush, and Layla's eyes traveled to the other side, landing on the brush. We were both frozen in shock. Did she just do that?

Next, Jen placed the hairbrush in Layla's left hand and asked her to show her what to do with it. Layla slowly lifted her only working arm and weakly started brushing the left side of her hair. She mostly brushed her face, yes, but it was clear she knew what to do. I started to wiggle next to Jeremiah. I wanted to loudly cheer her on, but he quickly grabbed me and reminded me we had to be silent.

Jen turned and asked for my ChapStick. She again placed it in Layla's left hand and asked if she knew what to do with it. And once again, Layla's left arm slowly raised to her lips as she attempted to put it on. Now, I was really wiggling, and Jeremiah was squeezing my arm before I erupted with cheers.

Jen was going to keep trying things until we reached a point where Layla could no longer perform the task. She handed Layla a pen and paper and asked if she knew what they did. Layla made an attempt to write, but she was weak and not a lefty. That didn't matter. The point was she clearly knew. That blank expression was deceiving; she was more awake than we realized.

Jen then wrote the words, "yes," and, "no," on a piece of paper and asked Layla to point to yes. Layla slowly pointed. She asked her to point to no, and again, Layla showed her. Identifying the words was one thing; even kindergarteners can pick out sight words. Did Layla know what those words meant? Jen followed up by asking Layla if she had three dogs at home. Layla pointed to the correct answer. She asked if she had two dogs at home, and again, Layla pointed to the right answer. She asked if she could write her dog's name and handed Layla that piece of paper and pen again. Layla tried but was not strong enough.

So, Jen grabbed an iPad and keyboard and asked if Layla could type her dog's name with her left hand. Jeremiah and I were sitting directly across from Layla and her team, so we were unable to see the iPad screen or what Layla was typing. It took a few minutes (that felt like hours!), but eventually, Jen turned the iPad toward us.

"Is your dog's name Kaia?" she asked.

We both had tears in our eyes as we shook our heads to confirm. I wanted to tackle them all with hugs. It was like they had found our Layla.

The therapy team seemed very pleased with Layla's results, too. She was done for the day, but she would have to do this three days in a row to be labeled as "emerged." The title simply meant she could tolerate longer, more intense therapies now and would begin the actual rehab. The part that concerned us wasn't her progress; it was the insurance. We came in under one program, and my insurance covered six weeks of it along with an additional sixty days of rehab. If Layla emerged a week into it, we were going to lose the other five weeks, and the sixty-day clock would begin. It didn't feel like enough time. She still had a long way to go, and we wanted her to get as much therapy as possible. We communicated these concerns to Jen and the team, but they did not seem as worried. They knew more than we realized: We were about to see something special happen with Layla.

Jen gave me the same instructions as Corrie did, "Let her rest." I wasn't supposed to keep pestering her with questions now that I knew she could communicate with yes and no. They returned Layla to her bed, and I think I made it a full 15 minutes before the suspense got the best of me. I needed to know if she was happy. I found a picture online of a green "yes" and a red "no" button and took a screen shot. My heart jumped out of my chest when Layla confirmed she was happy. This changed everything for me.

If she was happy, the challenges didn't matter anymore.
If she was happy, we would find our own version of living again, no matter what it looked like.
If she was happy, I was happy.

I should have stopped there, but it was hard. I wanted to see how much she remembered about her life. My daughter had a voice again, and we could make this work. We were limited to yes and no questions, but she could respond. That day she was able to tell me she had a sister and a brother, she was a cheerleader, she liked her hands rubbed, she did not like when I brushed her hair, and she loved Jesus. I even threw a few trick questions at her trying to see if she was paying attention, and she nailed it.

Layla was in there.

New terminology of the day: CRS for coma recovery scale. This test is used to track someone's progress and identify if they are emerging or not. It's like conscious vs. unconscious. When we left St Mary's, Layla wasn't doing much, only small movements on command, looking at us a little bit. Each day the changes are ever so small, especially sitting bedside and distracted with the parts you don't want to see. Since the day she arrived here, she was visibly very different, lots of moving and couldn't sit still. Today she decided she wanted us to notice. They took her for her first CRS test. It's nerve wracking for us, but Layla was always a good test taker, and she did not disappoint. We were stunned with each section of testing watching her do it. After we watched her identify various objects with her eyes, they moved on to handing her objects and asking what you do with them, like a hairbrush, ChapStick, pen and paper. She had no issues with any. She was even able to answer some yes/no questions and typed her dog's name. I can't even describe the emotions when she turned the screen and asked if that was our dog. Spinning is an understatement. She must do this three days consecutively to be considered "emerged," but I have absolute faith she will.

Day 25: Wednesday, June 15th

Now that we'd seen the CRS test, we had a better idea of what "emerged" looked like. They skip this part in the movies. We assumed she would wake up and be Layla again, or at least seem more functional. In reality, no one actually wakes up like that. When they said it was marathon, not a sprint, they weren't kidding. We were told she would see the greatest gains within the first two years. Mentally, I started the clock. We still had another 23 months. It helped keep me realistic and stopped me from rushing this. When you injure the fibers in your brain, they don't typically regenerate, but they can reorganize themselves. This is called neuroplasticity. Layla's injury was severe, there was a lot of reorganizing to do. Her brain was going to have to find new pathways to do everything again, and we had no certainty of what we would get back, only hope.

Every morning, someone would come by and drop off the day's schedule. They even scheduled times she would go back to bed for rest. I still didn't understand some of the abbreviations, so I would text Corrie for translation and my daily pep talk.

Me: What does this mean?

Corrie: She has occupational therapy for an hour and then speech therapy for thirty minutes after.

Me: I like her team so much.

120

Corrie: They are the best.

Me: Is it like a requirement to work here? Being amazing? Because you all are so amazing!

Corrie: LOL, remember those feelings when we upset you at some point.

I was really starting to love the people we interacted with at Shepherd. I couldn't imagine getting upset at any one of them! They were helping us find Layla again, or some version of her at least. I felt like I owed them everything. Most importantly, I trusted them.

Today, we did not accompany Layla for her CRS test. I think they were teaching Layla some independence (or maybe they were teaching us!). Jeremiah decided to take me downstairs to the cafeteria so I could navigate this without him one day. Five minutes in, I knew there was no way I was finding this place on my own. There are multiple elevators that lead to different places and one set of elevators that takes you to a whole other building. The cafeteria was located in the basement. You had to exit the elevator and take a few turns before getting there. I felt like we were in a maze where everything looked the same. He also took me to the coffee shop that was located on a whole different floor but a lot easier to find. You could get a real cup of coffee there—the complicated ones with flavors and funny names. Layla was going to love this place. She loved coffee. Her coffee order was always a mile long with specifications. She always said I was a boring coffee drinker; I drink it black. The coffee in the family breakroom wasn't great, but it served its purpose. This? This was a good cup of coffee. And it reminded me of home.

I had recently bought a coffee pot that grinds its own beans before brewing the coffee. I loved that machine. I woke up to the sounds of the grinder every day. I am typically the first one up in the house. Usually, I get a half hour alone with my coffee and my thoughts. Eventually, one of the kids would wander out of their room with their bedhead and PJs and begin filling the house with noise. It was our routine, and it was comforting. I missed it. I missed all the little things like that. You don't realize the little things you take for granted until they're gone, noisy kids and fancy coffee included.

Jen returned with Layla and gave us her progress report. Layla again performed and completed all the tasks asked of her. She worked some more with the iPad and keyboard and even wrote her name. She answered multiple questions for Jen and only got one wrong. When we asked what that question was, Jen replied, "She thought she had a brother." We all laughed when I informed them that she did, in fact, have a brother. Then I pointed out some of the pictures on the walls that included him and explained why he was not in Georgia with us. I can only imagine how frustrated Layla must've been when they didn't believe her. She never liked being wrong. It amused me to think of Layla not being able to argue her way out of something she knew was right. It made me wonder how much of her was inside screaming to be heard. You couldn't tell from the outside. She remained in the same expressionless state no matter what was going on around her.

Jeremiah and I were getting comfortable with the routine here. It seemed manageable. The schedule changed daily, but it mostly consisted of the same stuff in different orders. We were almost a week in at that point. Mentally, I was doing well, at least for now. Jeremiah was struggling a lot with Layla's right side being paralyzed. He was almost hyper focused on it. There were so many other things broken on her, but he really wanted her to move the right side. They had prepared us it may not come back. Just like everything else, nothing was guaranteed.

In fact, they prepared us for lots of things she may not get back or have to relearn, reading being amongst them. Reading and writing were Layla's favorite subjects in school. She could write the best stories. If you were lucky enough to get a birthday card from her, there was likely a short story written inside. A few times at Shepherd, I caught her looking at my phone while I was sending texts. To me, it appeared she was reading it, but we were told it was unlikely. Still, I had an idea. I wrote the words, "Raise your hand," on a piece of paper, and I started recording. I showed Layla the paper and up went her hand. I tried it again with, "Give me a thumbs up," and she did. Layla could definitely read. If she could read, then she could write. Maybe not now, but hopefully soon.

You had to have blind faith in this.
And eventually, that faith pays off.

Like when I returned to Cali that night, I received a video from Jeremiah: Layla could move her right foot.

The accident was on May 22nd. It's been 25 days since this started. Feels a lot longer. She's come so far in little bit of time and against the odds. We like to remind ourselves of the milestone dates. She first moved her fingers and toes on June 3rd, and she opened her eyes for the first time on May 31. Each milestone we keep resetting the goal line, grateful we got a little more than expected. Ultimately, I wanted her to be able to communicate. She was happy. I would love to hear her voice, but our system of thumbs up and down worked beautifully today. She told me she wanted music and when to skip the songs. She told me she likes her arms rubbed and definitely not her feet. (She always hated that!) She told me she had no pain today. She started turning her head a little today, and she can almost support it sitting up. Her back and neck are still very weak, and we are still waiting for her right side to move. We did see some movement in her right foot today, so maybe that's a start. We found out her jaw wires may come out in 2 weeks. In the meantime, they will begin trying to get her to speak with a special trach. I can't wait to hear her big mouth.

Day 26: Thursday, June 16th

The movement was minor, but it was just what Jeremiah needed. It was his opportunity to coach her the rest of the way. He was always up for these kinds of tasks.

Jeremiah was a total guy. He loved sports, and building things, and being outdoors. These were not things Layla particularly enjoyed, and Layla always demanded his attention. Over the years she had converted her manly sports dad into a cheer dad. She made him memorize routines and dances and taught him to speak in eight counts. He knew how to stunt her and spot her tumbling. He wore the team colors and spirit shirts and learned the songs. He would sit through a six-hour event to see his little girl perform for a little more than two minutes, and he would do it all over again the following weekend during cheer season. In ways, she had trained him for this exact thing. He was going to have to wait for her performance; he was going to have to coach her through it.

We had seen Layla compete dozens of times. The whole process was nerve wracking. She was a flyer—the girl being lifted in the stunts. When a stunt failed, you mostly remembered the flyer, something she took very seriously. If her stunt failed, it meant she failed. If a stunt dropped during a performance, the girls had to continue with a smile until the song was over. The routine would end, but that was when our job began. We would meet her on the sidelines to wipe her tears and attempt to find the right words to encourage her. This was a part of the sport she had chosen.

Stunts were bound to fall, but you had to finish with a smile and try again the next day. It was our job to coach her through the mental parts of it, just like we would have to do now.

Jessica was Layla's physical therapist. She was sweet and easy-going. We liked her. Honestly, we really liked everyone there. They all seemed to really love the work they were doing. They understood there would be bumps along the way, and they tried to keep our spirits up when they happened. Today, for example, Jessica tried getting Layla to stand, but she couldn't. She was too weak. Her brain hadn't figured out how to operate her legs and back. We were bummed about it, but Jessica said we would try another day. It was hard to imagine Layla not even being able to stand. Before, she could throw her body around in the most complex tumbling routines, and now, standing was too difficult. She didn't have any injuries related to physically being able to stand, but, like everything else, the brain ultimately controls what you can and cannot do. It's like the motherboard for every function of your body. It even controls healing. The wounds on her leg wouldn't even scab over because her brain wasn't telling them to. So, we just had to have hope for that neuroplasticity stuff to kick in.

Jen brought Layla back from her final day of CRS testing and announced Layla was officially emerged. Clearly, we knew this would happen after the last two successful days of testing. Layla once again answered all of Jen's questions correctly, except for one. Again, we asked what she got wrong. Layla had advanced to typing responses with Jen and when asked for her brother's name, she replied, "Jeremiah." We laughed and explained she was correct; I guess we should have mentioned he shared the same name with his dad. Typing her responses was limited to one-word answers. She wasn't at the point where she was formulating her own thoughts yet. It also took her a long time to type, and using her left hand wasn't helping. We decided to get her an iPad like the one Jen used. We figured maybe, in time, we could use it to communicate with her in case her voice never returned. We were trying to get creative.

That afternoon we worked on some new hand signals. She could successfully communicate sentiments like, "I love you," or "Hang loose," or "Peace," with her hands. More than that, she did this as a lefty now. Jeremiah is a lefty with certain things, so we thought maybe Layla could be, too. Maybe she could figure it out. It felt like a productive day. She couldn't stand, but she did so many other things. Tomorrow she would begin the rehab side of this, and her therapies would increase to three and a half hours.

Our 60-day clock was officially starting.

That made us nervous. When we were nervous, we got quiet, which made me more nervous. I knew we were going to need some form of therapy after all this was over. Even if it worked out, we were traumatized. I had been a frequent flyer with therapy, but Jeremiah was not, and I knew he wouldn't go willingly. So, I did what any obedient wife would do: I asked the Shepherd family therapist to ambush us in the room for a chat. The look he gave me spoke a thousand words. It didn't bother me because I knew he needed it. I knew *we* needed it. We finished up and scheduled a second meeting for Monday. I was going to have to get creative getting him to that one, but I would figure it out later.

Tonight, Cali needed me. She was having another difficult day.
It was time for another trip to the puppy store.

The thing that first scared me about Shepherd has become one of the things I love the most: the way they gave her independence from the start and treated her like she was not someone with a disability or injury. The staff talks to her and explains everything they are doing, even though she doesn't answer or even acknowledge them at times. Sometimes they just have conversations with her. I think part of the magic here is exactly that: the environment. I am a talker, especially when I'm nervous, and love to hear people's stories. Probably why I love reading what everyone shares on this page. I chat a lot with her nurses and therapists and love learning about them. A consistent thing I hear is how much they love working here and

126

how some were patients here themselves. You can really feel this is more than a paycheck to a lot of them. One of the therapists said something to me in the beginning that was hard to swallow then, but now I get it. She said, "I can't promise you Layla will progress the way you hope, but I can promise you we always end up with something beautiful." I think she meant my outlook more than Layla's progress. I get it now. So today, it's official, she is what they call "emerged." Does it mean she will hop out of bed tomorrow and do one of her dances? No. This means there's progress and something to celebrate. She was able to pick from multiple choices and answer questions like where she is, what kind of accident she was in, and what part of her was injured. I'm curious if she knows this from remembering or hearing us speak when we thought she couldn't hear us. We didn't press with more questions, not sure any of us are ready for that yet. Looking forward to the day we hear her voice again, and she can participate with us more. For now, we'll keep having fun with hand signals when she's in the mood. She also reaches for us and just wants to hold hands or have her hands rubbed. It's adorable. Please keep praying for her right side.

Day 27: Friday, June 17th

If we thought she was restless before, we had no idea what was coming. Her poor little body seemed like it was in overdrive. She kept repeating the same involuntary movements with her left leg, and her hand was going up and down, grabbing at things aimlessly. Now, she had a different look on her face, too. It resembled anger or frustration. Her eyes seemed frantic and wild at times, and she would search our faces as if looking for us to help her. They prepared us for what her being a 4 looked like, so we were ready for her worst. For once, there was a benefit to her not being able to speak. We could hear other patients in the same stage yelling in the halls, one even begging for help. Their cries were painful. You could feel the confusion and distress in their words. All we could do was pray for them, so, we did. We prayed for comfort and peace for those we heard on the hall, and we prayed that Layla would pass through this stage quickly. She had it easy compared to the others, at least that's how it looked to us. She also had us at her side, while many others didn't. If a patient was left unattended, they had to be restrained. We tried to avoid needing the restraints as much as possible by staying with Layla around the clock. At night, though, we had no choice on the matter of the restraints. She didn't always sleep, so the restraints protected her. Unfortunately, when she didn't sleep, we didn't either.

Me: Morning.

Jeremiah: Morning, rough night. Went to bed around 5.

Me: Why!? You want me to stay tonight? I just need to prepare Cali for that.

Jeremiah: Yes, I must sleep, like a long sleep. I am beyond tired.

Me: OK perfect, I will get ready.

Jeremiah: She stays up all night fidgety. It was the toughest night since ICU in terms of sleep.

Me: My poor Layla. I'm grabbing your food then heading your way. I'll be there before her shower. Try to nap. She's probably tired, too.

Jeremiah: The sooner the better.

Layla had earned herself some specialty restraints, one being a cast for her left arm that kept it straight so she couldn't reach her trach. The restraints seemed to make her angrier, so we tried to find ways to distract her. In a normal day, she would have been on her phone talking to friends. She wasn't able to do that yet, and I had locked her phone out trying to guess her password. We did have the new iPad now. I had asked friends and family to send her video messages for the day she was ready to watch them, and today felt like a good day for that.

Her attention span was only a few minutes before we had to move on to something else. In between transitions, she would grab my hand and squeeze it with that look in her eyes. It was borderline aggressive. If you could scream with a look, she was doing it. She was frustrated and wanted me to fix it, but I couldn't. I knew she had to go through this stage before getting to the next one. I was hoping it was the peak, and she would start to calm down. We spent the better part of the day in this cycle. As much as I wanted to break down, I didn't, but I was walking a fine line. I hated not being able to give her relief. I wondered what was going on in her head—if her thoughts sounded like the man screaming down the hall. Finally, the nurse arrived to give her the sleep meds at 9:00, and I knew I could lay down afterward.

That was until I realized the chair had to be converted to the bed. Just like at St. Mary's, I couldn't figure it out. I sat on the chair and started laughing at myself. This time I was brave enough to ask for help before a repeat incident of last time.

Jeremiah: I forgot to open the chair for you. Did you get it back down?

Me: I was just dealing with that, lol.

Jeremiah: Don't make me call the nurse's station.

Me: It's down, they helped me.

Jeremiah: Send me a pic.

Me: It's dark, and she's asleep.

Jeremiah: I'm callin. I don't believe you. Send me a pic or I'm calling nurse's station.

He knows me so well.

This time, I had asked for help though. This entire experience was teaching me to do that more often. Jeremiah and I were terrible at asking for help, even when we needed it. We had no choice but to accept it now. We needed help with so many things, and I know there was a lesson in it for us. We typically liked to be the ones on the other end of helping. We were learning that receiving help was okay too—that being vulnerable was a good thing for us. Helping others was always very rewarding, but by denying others the ability to help us, it was like throwing their gift in the trash.

Lesson learned.

If you remember previously, I explained that Rancho scale. Layla is at about a 4. So far, we've been lucky she isn't really showing signs of too much aggression, just the restlessness. It's a little sad to watch. She just can't sit still and hardly sleeps. The left hand and leg move constantly. Ultimately, it's a good thing, and we are happy to see it. I just feel bad for her. She also goes after things she's not supposed to touch, like stomach tube and trach. She's pulled a few things out and handed them to us. She's maneuvered her way out of tons of their restraints (they call her Houdini) and even had a special cast made for her to make her less reachy. She's doing all this with one working side; I'm almost afraid to see what happens with both. She was pretty tired during speech therapy. Kept pointing to the word "tired," so they didn't push her too hard. I think she had a big week and earned the weekend off. So, for now we do puzzles on the iPad.

Day 28: Saturday, June 18th

Usually, our day started at 7:00 am sharp. Weekends were different here. She would only have a couple therapies, and they started later. I was looking forward to a quiet day, hoping the restlessness would subside a little. She seemed calmer to me, but maybe she was just exhausted.

Jeremiah: Morning, how's it going?

Me: Morning, just had PT.

Jeremiah: How'd she do?

Me: First ten minutes was waking her up. She was out cold.

Jeremiah: Why does she go into states of unconsciousness still?

Me: She's just sleeping, babe. She's telling me so many things with the yes and no. She told me she can feel me touching her right side. I pressed all the way up her arm.

Jeremiah: That's awesome. What's the plan? You want to stay another night?

Me: Sure, just let me know.

Jeremiah: Scratch that. Cali's not having it. She wants you. I even took her to several parks, but she only wants her momma.

Me: I'm not ready. Wait a little.

Layla was done with therapies by noon that day, and I had so many questions for her. Since it was a quieter day, I thought it was a good chance to chat. After her nap, the nurse returned her to the wheelchair and left me with the job of tilting her every 20 minutes. I used this time to ask Layla questions and practice more with her hands. She seemed more annoyed with me than usual and kept shifting her eyes to the bed. She clearly was not happy about being moved in the first place. She would look at the bed and then back at me repeatedly. It seemed like she was trying to tell me what she wanted. It's not like I could get her there without help, so I continued with my questions until she picked her back and head up off the wheelchair in an attempt to stand up. I couldn't believe it. She couldn't even nod her head, and now, she was supporting it and trying to stand. She could only get as far as the lap restraint allowed, but she was determined. Each time I would ask her to lay back, she would, but it didn't last long. She would keep attempting this for an hour until I finally called a nurse for help. She got her wish and returned to bed.

Layla was always relentless when she wanted her way.

So, it appears today the restlessness is moving in the right direction, and she seemed slightly calmer. She did have me up around 5:30 this morning doing puzzles and listening to music, but then she rolled herself over (another new skill) and put herself back to sleep. She had a short physical therapy session followed by occupational therapy. They were working on her neck supporting her head and head control, which she really had none of at this point. They were also working on the right side, still not much going on yet either. Around 1:00 they moved her to a wheelchair with restraints (since she finds ways out of things) and left me alone with her. We did more of the yes/no questions. Those are always fun. She then decided she was over the chair, fully started picking up her back off the chair and supporting neck and head for the first time! If it wasn't for the restraints, I think she would have tried standing. After the shock of what she was doing and getting her slowly back into place, the girl kept doing it! She added some thumbs down letting me know she was not happy with me and kept looking at the bed. I finally asked if she was trying to stand up, and she pointed to yes. There was no one qualified around to execute her standing plan, so I kept explaining this was not safe and we had to wait till Monday at PT. More thumbs down and trying to get up. I finally called the nurse to help me get her back to bed safely with the lift. The nurses are so sweet, and she's already won them over. They loved seeing her determination to stand. After we got her to bed, she remembered her new trick and was trying to sit up and swing her working leg over the edge. She officially has a new bed restraint to add to her collection.

Day 29: Sunday, June 19th

There are not many other places Jeremiah would have rather been than at Layla's bedside, which is where he woke up that Father's Day morning. I hit a bakery on the way to the hospital and brought him a multitude of treats to help celebrate. We had a calm day planned with zero therapies and only family time.

She was getting more mobile in the bed and could turn over and sleep on her side now. Seeing her curled up on her side meant something to us. You could almost forget the injury seeing her like that. She looked so much like her former self. And just like her former self, her personality was starting to show. Layla was always a cuddler. She couldn't get enough physical touch. I was not built that way, and I often had to remind myself how much she needed it. That day I made a joke that I was going to crawl into her hospital bed with her and squeeze her. We had never physically gotten in her bed before. To my surprise, she used her new skill and scooted over to make room for me, patting the bed next to her with her left hand. So, I kicked off my shoes and crawled in the bed. She grabbed my arm and turned over, pulling me close. There aren't many words that can adequately describe how that moment felt. I was finally getting to hug her again, remembering how I didn't hug her enough before all this. It was another one of those thoughts that haunted me. I knew then I would be spending a lot of time in this bed with her. I made myself a promise I would work on that, too, adding it to my ever-growing list.

135

That evening I had plans to take Cali to dinner. I felt terrible this was how Jeremiah would be spending Father's Day, but he insisted with Layla was where he wanted to be. Shortly after I left, he texted me a photo of a cake and large bowl of fruit.

Me: Who did that!?

Jeremiah: Someone who knows strawberries and kiwi are my favorite.

Me: It's not me? No one even asked me, I swear.

Jeremiah: I don't know. It just was dropped in the room, no note.

Me: I thought I was the only one who knew the fruit thing.

Jeremiah: Very kind of someone, for sure.

A little while later he sent a video of Layla. She was finally moving her right leg. This meant everything to him. He had been tirelessly working on it with her. You could hear the tears in his voice as he encouraged her in the video. It was the best Father's Day gift she could have given him. It was almost as if she waited for this exact day and this exact moment when they were alone.

Me: NO WAY! Well nurse Rogan, you can add physical therapist to your titles!

Jeremiah: Her right-side works, I can't believe it.

Me: Happy Father's Day.

Jeremiah: Did you know they have a Houston's around the corner?

Me: Why? You wanna take me on a date?

136

Jeremiah: Ya, but I'm having trouble getting a babysitter.

Me: So... you're saying you're a guy with baggage.

When I met Jeremiah, I was working at a Houston's restaurant. I also had a second job, and I was a full-time student. He lived 45 minutes away from me, but we always found ways to make it work. Fast forward a few years, and we lived in Palm Beach together. He proposed to me at a Houston's owned restaurant. Now, Houston's was one of our favorite places to eat. We hadn't been there in forever, and just hearing him mention it brought me back to that moment when he proposed. I was so dumbfounded when he did it that I didn't answer right away. I started making small talk while he waited on one knee, getting stepped on by servers trying to get by. I ramble on when I'm nervous, but he always has a way of bringing me back to the moment. That night, when he finally got me to focus on the question at hand, I said an enthusiastic, "yes!"

And the rest was history.

Every day God has given us a little more than we ever expected. I guess the same applies to my life in general. In the beginning, we were told how serious this was and warned of the slim chances of survival. God delivered. We were told she likely would not progress more than the girl lying there with machines breathing for her and eyes closed. She started to breathe and opened her eyes. We were warned countless times there's no guarantee she will ever progress to the next step, she fights and progresses every. single. day. There are only so many things you can call luck or coincidence; this is clearly God at work. I can't even comprehend it. I prepared myself mentally for the outcome being whatever we had up until that moment. I had peace with that even; my girl was alive after all. I prepared myself that the changes would be slow and minor if at all, told myself this would be a marathon not a sprint, and she amazes us daily with these huge steps. 5 days ago, while I celebrated her being able to say yes and no, someone special shared the verse from

Ephesians 3:20 about God giving us more then we asked or imagined. I didn't imagine I would get this much "Layla" back. I knew what those scans said; I knew what the doctors said. I really tried to keep realistic expectations. And I knew this was going to take a ton of prayers. More than I asked or imagined, that's what I keep getting. More prayers from family, friends, and strangers than I ever imagined. People who stormed heaven's gates for Layla. More than I could have asked for or imagined. My heart is so full.

Day 30: Monday, June 20th

Before this, I don't know that I ever actually believed in miracles. I believed the impossible could happen, but I also thought it may be hyped up a bit when it does. I knew the Bible stories, but I thought that stuff didn't happen in real life—not to me anyways. I had seen movies and over-dramatized news stories with amazing endings to tragic stories. I didn't trust any of these were accurate. They seemed inflated for entertainment. I wanted to believe them, but it was difficult for me without seeing it firsthand.

When I arrived at the hospital that morning, Layla was already in her chair. She looked annoyed, and Jeremiah looked tired. She had obviously been giving him a hard time. I approached her wheelchair, and she leaned into my body and held on to me with her left arm. I was surprised by this. She didn't typically do things without being asked. This she was doing on instinct, like she wanted her momma. It made me emotional. This was not typical Layla behavior. Before the accident, me and Layla butted heads a lot. In many ways we were very much the same person, and we clashed because of it. It was expected at her age, and I knew we had to ride out the season of teenage years. But today? This felt like my Layla before those teenage years hit. This felt like my little girl who didn't challenge every word I said and just wanted to be near me. This felt like a situation I could fix with kisses. I soaked it up as long as I could before the therapy team arrived and interrupted our moment.

Lucky for me, Jeremiah forgot about our own therapy session we scheduled for today. We had an appointment during Layla's physical therapy. I fed him first, then reminded him we had some trauma therapy to do. There was no escaping it. After an eye roll and a few complaints, he dragged his feet alongside me to the counselor's office. It's not that he had anything against therapy; he just didn't like it for himself. Even opening up to me was challenging for him sometimes, but if you got him talking, the floodgates would open. I knew this, so I knew how to steer our session there.

The first few minutes he spent giving me a lot of those looks—the ones that say everything without saying anything. He wasn't budging. He was not in the mood to open up to this woman. I was going to have to trigger him.

So, I told the therapist our situation was hard, but something beautiful was coming out of it. That did it. Jeremiah did not think there was anything beautiful about seeing his daughter like this. It's not that I did either. I was speaking more about the hearts being changed because of her story. His focus was only Layla. It pained him to think of the struggles she was going to have or the things she would lose. He was not only grieving for himself, but for the life Layla lost that day. We didn't know what surviving would even look like. Would she ever go to college like she planned? Could she even finish high school? Would she ever cheer again? Would we hear her voice or see her walk ever again? He finally started venting.

A knock at the door interrupted us. It seemed strange that someone would interrupt a therapy session, right? It was Layla's physical therapist, Jessica, standing in the door with an apologetic look on her face.

"Sorry to interrupt," she said excitedly, "but I was wondering if you wanted to see your daughter walk."

If I didn't believe in miracles before, I would after this. It didn't seem possible she was talking about our daughter. Layla couldn't even stand. Layla needed a special lift to transfer her out of the bed. Layla just started moving her right leg the night before. Jeremiah and I jumped out of our seats and followed Jessica. Even our counselor followed; she had to see it too!

"How is this possible?" I kept saying as we made our way to our girl.

Part of me thought she had the wrong family, at least until we saw her. Jessica led us to one of the empty hallways near the elevators. Layla was sitting in her wheelchair at one end with another therapist waiting for us. She had her usual blank expression, only she looked more tired now. Jessica noticed, too, and promised Layla this would be the last time. Layla nodded her head in agreement. That was the first time we saw her do that. Before I could celebrate the head nod, Jessica helped Layla stand up out of the wheelchair. She was standing! She was on her own two feet! Before we could fully take that in, they began. Jessica was in a rolling stool next to her, guiding the right foot into place with each step while the other therapist held her left hand for support. Her right arm hung uselessly at her other side. They began their slow march down the hallway toward us. We watched in awe as Layla's little body pushed through each step. She had lost so much weight and standing made that more obvious. Her knees seemed too big for the skinny legs they were attached to. And we couldn't take our eyes off her.

We were spinning.
We were celebrating.
We were crying.
Layla could walk!

Layla was allowed to return to bed as promised and get a much-needed nap. Instead of using the lift, Jessica showed us how to stand and pivot Layla, then slowly lower her back into bed. This would be the way we transferred her between bed and wheelchair from then on. We were so glad to get rid of that lift. The lift reminded us how injured she was.

It was a lot to look at, not to mention difficult for us to operate without help. This was the first task we were cleared to do with Layla. Whenever you were cleared for something, you had to perform the task in front of a qualified person. So now, instead of waiting for nurses, we could get her ready in her wheelchair for her scheduled therapies. It was just a "stand-pivot-sit," but it made us so happy. As usual, Layla seemed indifferent.

While Layla slept, we took the opportunity to update our family and friends. I didn't even prepare them for what they were about to see. I still had no words to describe it. They'd have to see it to believe it, just like me. I sent the video and waited. With each response, we celebrated all over again. Seeing Layla walk was surreal. This was a miracle. I finally understood what that meant. I would never doubt miracles again.

Eventually, it was time to share with her Facebook page; they were part of this too. I posted the video with the only caption that felt right: *"Are you ready for a miracle?"*

Day 31: Tuesday, June 21st

Layla was getting some new jewelry today. Jen would be putting a speaking valve on Layla's tracheotomy and working with Layla to find her voice again. We were so anxious to hear that voice! It wasn't going to be easy, but it was possible and that's all we needed to know.

A speaking valve lets air into the tube, then closes, so the air goes out your nose and mouth. Speech happens when air passes over your vocal cords. With a tracheotomy, a lot of the air passes through the tracheotomy tube rather than over the cords. Layla would have to push air hard enough to get it there. That in itself is difficult after a brain injury. Now, add the extra obstacle of her jaw being wired, and it's that much harder. There was another challenge: Layla's stoma. A stoma is the actual incision or opening the tracheotomy fits into, and Layla's kept opening wider each day. It was becoming an issue that would eventually require stitches. You could often hear air escaping it when she coughed. All that combined meant one thing: Speaking was going to be tricky.

We waited in the room while she went for her therapies. Jessica was doing physical therapy first, followed by speech with Jen. We were afraid to leave in the event she did something big like the previous day. Still, Jeremiah was also exhausted and needed sleep. It wasn't easy sleeping there, and he had taken the last two consecutive nights. I tucked him into the little chair for a nap while I tried to get some work done. About an hour later, Jessica popped her head in the door. She wanted to bring me an update: Layla had been moving her right arm during therapy. As much as I wanted to jump up and scream, I didn't. I wanted Jeremiah to sleep and figured it would be a nice surprise for him when he woke up. It felt like we were checking things off a list, leaving the biggest thing for last.

Where would she be cognitively at the end of this?

Layla was not able to speak during speech therapy that day, but I felt peace about it. It was only her first attempt. It took her a month to be able to use her right arm, so maybe she just needed more time. Her last therapy for the day was occupational with Emily, and I was being signed off to shower her without assistance. I was no longer nervous about getting the trach wet. It's amazing how we were getting more comfortable with her care each day. It also made it a lot easier not having to use the lift. It helped having the therapists there encouraging me, too. They were not only helping Layla, but they were helping us. They were our guides and teachers. It wasn't mandatory you had to learn this stuff, but we wanted to and I think they appreciated that. Once you reach your discharge date, they provide family training tailored to where your person is at that point. This way, you are equipped to care for them before getting home. But we wanted to learn all the stuff leading up to that point. We wanted to be able to care for her along the way; we wanted to be part of her healing. To us, it was a way to show her how much we loved her, even if she didn't understand. Most kids will never understand their parent's love anyway.

Layla was starting to recognize something was wrong with her mouth. She would use her fingers to explore the wires in her jaw, and we had to constantly stop her from messing with them. She knew she could get me in her bed now and constantly requested it by patting the mattress next to her side. I would use my phone camera as a mirror to show her what was wrong with her teeth and explain her jaw was wired now but wouldn't be forever. She seemed curious at seeing her face in the camera, sometimes even sad. Her eyebrows even started pulling downward, which gave me a strange comfort. It's not that we wanted her sad, but sad was at least an emotion. It was nice to see something resemble a normal reaction; it was nice to see her face move a little more.

Jeremiah's time with us was ending soon. He would have to go home in a week. He was trying to get as much time with her as possible. I know it killed him to leave her, especially because we weren't sure how long it would be. We had somewhat of a plan. Originally Cali was supposed to stay with me, but we soon realized how impossible that would be. It was too difficult for her. She wanted at least one parent, and I would need to stay full time in the hospital with Layla. So, she asked to return home with her dad. I was honestly surprised by this. Looks like we would both be missing a daughter! They would go home and make weekend flights up when possible. Shepherd Center had family housing on the property we could stay in if needed, plus we had Bethany's. There was no way to make a concrete plan because so much depended on Layla. Our plan, for the moment, was for each of us to soak up as much time with the daughter we would be leaving as possible.

Me: How are you?

Jeremiah: Wishing the week would slow down. Just sitting next to the bed watching her sleep.

Me: I'm praying it goes fast. You are getting the chance to bring comfort to Cali, which is equally important right now. I'd almost say it's harder.

Jeremiah: I'm also praying for the man down the hall yelling every two minutes. Poor guy screamed all night, and he's still screaming.

Me: I know, it's really sad.

Jeremiah: I feel like that would have been her if we left her alone, like the mind knows nurture versus nature.

145

Day 32: Wednesday, June 22nd

With brain injury, it's common to take steps backwards. It's expected even. They prepared us for it many times. But Layla had been charging forward without setbacks, so it was easy for us to get greedy. In fact, that almost made the setbacks tougher when they came.

Today, they came.

Layla had an old friend appear: her migraines. She couldn't verbally communicate, so she just gripped the left side of face and curled into a little ball. She hadn't shown reactions to pain before that. At bedtime, they would come in and give her an injection in her stomach, and she never flinched. She just sat still and unimpressed. On one hand, it was a good thing to see her feeling something, but on the other, we knew how these typically ended: with vomit. Throwing up with a wired jaw and tracheotomy was dangerous, so everyone was on eggshells. It was brutal watching her suffer—as if she hadn't been through enough. They were trying different medications, but nothing seemed to work. We tried some of our usual tricks, like ice packs and massages. It was a seven-hour waiting game until she finally fell asleep.

When I left the hospital that night, I was frustrated. I didn't like seeing her suffer. I knew how these migraines interrupted our life before. Why couldn't they just go away? Or at least wait until the wires came off? My son called me on the ride home. I could hear the stress in his voice. We

146

used to talk every day, and now, we were restricted to the few moments I had between other things. He needed me more present. Cali needed me more present, too. He was holding back as to not worry me, but I could hear it. I was holding back telling him how hard this was, but I'm sure he knew as well. I hated how distant he felt.

I was typically good at compartmentalizing, almost too good. I could separate my feelings and thoughts and deal with them when I wanted. It was a blessing and a curse. It allowed me to focus on the present without letting the past interfere or disrupt my emotions. It also meant I could tuck those emotions way down and never deal with them. Not this though. I couldn't stand the idea of my kids hurting. I felt like I was choking, trying to stuff the way I felt down and pretend like everything was fine.

It was not fine.
I was not fine.
 I was starting to crack… again.

Jeremiah: Whatcha doin'?

Me: Writing my Facebook post. I'm trying to sound happy, but I'm not.

Jeremiah: Why are you trying to sound happy, but you're not?

Me: I'm worried about the migraines. I'm worried about the catheter. I'm worried about the large hole in her chest that keeps getting bigger. I want her to have some relief. I just booked your plane tickets, and I'm sad about that. I already miss Cali. I feel like a terrible mom who can't take care of her kids. I don't talk to our son enough anymore. I feel like I'm being pulled in too many different directions, and I am failing at everything. I keep forgetting stuff.

Jeremiah: You are being pulled in many different directions, but that's what makes you a great mom. You're looking at it all wrong.

Me: Well, I feel like I'm sucking at everything.
Jeremiah: That's not true. Turn this around.

Me: And I'm scared of everything. I'm so tired of being scared of everything.

Jeremiah: Those are valid worries, but step back and think. Our worry used to be: Will she be alive when that helicopter lands? Will she ever wake up? Will she make it through the night? Those are worries.
It's okay to be worried, but look at the whole picture. There's a couple down the hall that are flying home soon with their son still in a coma. You can worry, but don't forget to be thankful and don't let the devil poke holes in your happiness.

Me: You're right. I'm sorry, it's wearing on me a little today.

Jeremiah: You're having a moment where you are forgetting how blessed we are.

Me: I know I'm blessed. I just want my kids to be okay.

Jeremiah: Take a deep breath. You're doing a good job.

Sometimes it's okay to not be okay. Sometimes you need someone to remind you. Sometimes you need to cry, or yell, or hide. Then, you can try again tomorrow.

Good news! Wires are getting removed this Tuesday at noon! This should be her last surgery and will hopefully help get her to speak again. They do the surgery at the hospital next door, and there's some secret tunnel she is transported through. I don't know why that sounded neat to me. Her speech therapist has been working with her this week on speaking and figuring out how to use those vocal cords again, but she hasn't quite found her voice yet. Today started great. She did amazing in

148

physical therapy, occupational therapy, speech, and some evaluation thing. We don't usually get to witness it; we just hear about it after. It's great to see how excited the therapists look. We were cleared to remove her from the bed and into the wheelchair on our own this week, and I was cleared to give her unsupervised showers. (It's harder than you think!) Unfortunately, Layla's therapies were cut short today due to a migraine. She's had them since she was very little and usually ends up with vomit. Before the accident she would get them a few times a month. I had really hoped maybe they'd stay at bay during this, but we saw that familiar look on her face around 1:00 and knew it was coming. They tried a few medications to help, but nothing worked, not even the strong stuff! So, we laid in bed scratching her head, rubbing her feet, applying ice, and praying she didn't get sick with a wired jaw. She looked pretty helpless and obviously in pain, but she made it to the 9:30 sleep meds, didn't get sick, and has been sleeping since, so that's a win. Tomorrow is a new day.

Day 33: Thursday, June 23rd

I usually started the day asking Layla the same two questions:

Are you happy?
Are you in pain?

She was happy, and the headache was gone today. We had index cards for her to explain other emotions, like tired or uncomfortable. Now, I wanted to try some typing with her. I wanted to be able to have a conversation with her, and I wanted to see how much she remembered about who she was before. I opened the Notes app in my phone and gave it to Layla. I explained to her that I would ask questions, and she could type her responses there. She was able to tell me her age, her birthday, a few of her friends' names, and her favorite food. She was typing with her left hand. Her right hand worked but not well. It was very weak in comparison to the left; her entire right side was weaker. The goal was to make her use the right side as much as possible, almost waking it up. She often resisted this. She knew the quicker way for everything was to use the better-working left side. We even started making her use her feet to push her wheelchair. She gave us attitude about it, but attitude was a good sign. Cognitively she knew we were pushing her. It felt like we were moving into a new stage with her. Originally, we were learning to care for her basic needs, but now, we would partake in helping her rehabilitate.

They were training us to walk independently with her and suggested we practiced as much as she would tolerate. For a girl with little facial expressions, she made it clear when she didn't want to do something. Walking practice was not her favorite thing. When she didn't like something, we got a thumbs down and a dirty look. To go on walks, we had to get her into the wheelchair and bring her to that same hallway. With the help of a gait belt, we would stand her up and guide her to the end of the hallway. It took a lot out of her. It took a lot out of us, too. We were restricted to the hallway on her floor, so we would have her walk up and down a few times before returning to her bed. She would go as fast as she could manage to get it over with, and there were times she was hard to keep up with. Her speed made everyone laugh.

She had come a long way from the girl trapped in bed.

I know many of you have shared how our situation has changed you, and I am right there with you. It's changed me, too. It's made so many things I thought were important before seem insignificant now. It's taught me to slow down and be patient. It's made me want to cherish every second I get with my kids. It's shown me how great the world can be. It's made me realize I am not in control, and I don't need to be. And it's reminded me that God never fails me. I know technically I'm in a bad situation, but it's also such a beautiful one. Today was more of the usual. Lots of therapies! She did well and even climbed some stairs. She's also getting so good at standing and transferring from bed to chair. She got another headache today but didn't seem as bad as yesterday. She was a trooper. The right side gets stronger each day. She typically uses the left arm to move the right, so we are trying to break the habit by holding her left and asking her to do things with the right. She definitely doesn't enjoy it and will even eye roll, but I like it. It's very Layla.

Day 34: Friday, June 24th

It seemed like overnight, Layla learned how to text again. She was always nosey about what we were doing on our phones, but now, she was taking it upon herself to respond to our text messages. Her responses were brief and usually in the right context. She answered some of my work messages even. You had to watch her, though, because the conversation quickly turned dark. Sometimes she'd ask if she was dead. Clearly, she was in a very confused state.

To make it worse, her memory was only a few minutes long. Soon, she'd be repeating the same questions all over again. It almost seemed like being trapped in a bad dream. As much as we wanted to hear what she was thinking, it was also disturbing. We were in this cycle with her most of the day.

Each time she asked if she was alive, we assured her she was.
Each time she wanted to know what happened, we lightly explained it.
Each time she wanted to know what she had to do to get out, we encouraged her to be patient and work hard.

It was around this time she also started recognizing when I left, and she didn't like it. I only had the weekend to enjoy Cali before she returned to Florida with Jeremiah. Usually, I spent the better part of the day at Shepherd, and one of the cousins would entertain Cali until I got home. Since Cali was leaving Monday, I was leaving the hospital a little earlier now.

That day, I had just left Layla and was still in the parking garage when I got my first text from her iPad.

Layla: Hi.

Me: Hi Layla, I love you.

Layla: How long?

Me: Not long, I just have to spend some time with Cali.

Layla: OK

Me: I love you so much.

Layla: Turn around.

Me: Why? Do you need me to come back?

Layla: I miss you.

Me: Aww baby I miss you too. I won't be gone long, I promise.

Layla: See you soon.

Me: Very soon. I love you Layla.

Layla: I love you.

It was the first time I heard her verbalize an emotion like that without being prompted. She missed me. Something about it felt so good. It was definitely better than seeing her in fear about whether she was alive or not. I wondered if she really understood what it meant. Layla did not typically say she missed us. Even as a child, Layla was never very clingy. The day I dropped her at her pre-K classroom, all the kids were clinging to their mothers and sobbing before going inside. I honestly felt left out. My Layla was standing confidently, pulling away from me trying to be released from my grip. I bent down to her eye level and explained it was okay to cry or be scared. She looked at me like I had three heads.

"I'm not a baby, Mom," she said boldly. "I'll see you after school."

In she marched without looking back. Sometimes it felt like Layla skipped over childhood all together.

Apologies to anyone Layla texted from my phone today and made me sound crazy. Just kidding, I know you loved it. She took it upon herself to answer a lot of my text messages today. Some of them she announced it was her and had a small conversation. I can confidently say she can read and write. She also Face Timed Amanda at work, and I had no idea until I heard the ringing. We just had such a fun day. She's there but not there if that makes sense. She also started typing me questions. This is a new skill. She mostly wanted to know when the accident happened. She was asking why the days feel so long and repeatedly asked when we can leave. There is definitely a lot of confusion in her questions, and I'm sure this is hard to sort through. She typed multiple times, "But I am fine," and tried to convince me it's time to go home. I explained there's a lot of work to do, like operations, and walking better, and learning to do everyday things. We were getting trained and certified on walking independently with her, and she decided we should speed walk. Remember that first walking video? This is much different. God is so good.

Day 35: Saturday, June 25th

Layla didn't always text from the iPad. She would text from anything she could get her hands on. We had to hide devices from her. It was a bit obsessive compulsive. Once she was caught texting from Jeremiah's Apple Watch when he fell asleep next to her. If she was awake and not in therapy, she was texting or trying to. The majority of her texts were going to me. If I was with her, we used the text thread to communicate. I would answer verbally, and she would speak through the text screen on the phone. If I was away, she would text me from Jeremiah's phone or her iPad. Since we could only speak this way, we had documentation of what her thoughts looked like. It all seemed very confusing and scary for her. It made me wonder if this was why the man down the hall screamed for help so much.

Layla: Hi.

Me: Hi, is this Layla?

Layla: Yes

Me: I'll be there soon.

Layla: OK

Me: I love you.

Layla: I love you.

Me: Did you have a good night?

Jeremiah: Yes, Dad's great. I'm gonna miss him when he leaves, hope you will be as cool as Dad.

Me: Ha Ha babe

Jeremiah: Someone has become obsessed with wanting my phone.

Me: Give it to her.

Layla: Am I dead?

Me: No baby. You are very much alive and safe.

Layla: Where am I?

Me: You are at a hospital in Georgia to make you better.

Layla: Am I getting better?

Me: You are getting better every day. You are safe, you are protected, you are loved, and you are healed.

Layla: How much longer?

Me: Maybe 5 weeks? End of July?

Layla: I don't like it here.

Me: Its OK baby, it will go fast.

Layla: It's not going fast.

Me: It just feels that way today. Want me to bring books and paints?

Layla: Yes. The days are replaying.

Me: I know it feels that way.

It was troubling seeing her so confused. All we could do was comfort her and pray she would phase out of this stage. I wanted her to be able to converse with her sister eventually—to give Cali some peace that her sister was okay. I was worried this version of Layla would have upset her. Kerry and Mary Jane took Cali that day, so I could be at Shepherd. We were being signed off to independently walk with Layla, and they had plans to go hiking and do some baking with Cali while I was gone. I would meet them later, and I was looking forward to it. Seeing them brought me comfort, and I knew it was the same for Cali.

The Georgia family had been keeping Cali very busy. They took her to every attraction in the Atlanta area. They filled her time with activities and distractions—anything to see her smile. Bethany took her to pools and summer camps. Mary Jane's youngest daughter, Sarah, took her to a butterfly garden. One of the days, Jessica had her make a summer bucket list and proceeded to conquer the majority of the list in a day. Tomorrow would be my last day with her. When I asked her what she wanted to do, her response made me laugh.

"Honestly, you guys are exhausting me. Can we just stay home and do nothing?"

That night, I went to pick her up for the evening. I always loved the drive to Mary Jane's house. It looked like something out of a car commercial, with rolling hills, and winding roads, and trees for miles. I had never done this drive on my own before; usually Jeremiah drove us. I was nervous about driving on those hills. As it turned out, it was actually pretty soothing, and I mentally kicked myself for not trying it sooner. It felt like something Jenna would have been proud of me for. I was pretty proud of me. I successfully navigated myself right into their driveway without any issues. I was starting to realize my fears weren't as scary as I imagined. Maybe they've even been holding me back from living at times.

I loved coming here. My kids loved it, too. Certain homes you walk in and just feel peace, and Mary Jane and Kerry's home was that. I was grateful we were getting this time with them. Cali was excited to show me the zucchini bread she had made with Mary Jane. I would make that at home, too. It was Mary Jane's recipe, which a lot of my recipes came from her. Each one of my children had a favorite food that came from Mary Jane's recipes. Zucchini bread was my son's, Layla loved tiramisu, and Cali's was her chicken soup. She called it "magic soup" because she said it made everything feel better. Whenever the kids had any sign of a cold, I made that soup. I think the magic was in the love behind it, passed to me from Mary Jane to them.

Shepherd Center only allowed four visitors on our list, and Jeremiah and I were two of them. We had to choose them before we arrived and submit paperwork. Mary Jane and Kerry were the other two. Once Jeremiah went home, I was going to need them a lot more. Once he was gone, I would be moving into her room without any end date and no intention of leaving her side. It was almost like glamping. I had a washer and dryer a few doors down, and the room was stocked with a few things I would need daily. We had our own bathroom. There was a cafeteria downstairs and crappy coffee down the hall. I was taken care of, but the thing I needed most was their company time to time. Layla was not a great conversationalist, so it was nice getting visitors. They would also be driving Cali and Jeremiah to the airport on Monday. We discussed details over dinner, ready to begin the next phase of this.

The original plan here was for Cali to remain in Georgia with me when Jeremiah goes home. She is surrounded by family here who will do anything to see her smile. Unfortunately, I think the absence of her parents and sister and the added fear of sleeping away from us are too much. She has decided to return home with Dad on Monday. It's not going to be easy for any of us. I will miss her incredibly, and her dad will have a big job supporting and caring for her. Her Georgia family will really miss her, especially the younger cousins who have grown to love her. We knew this wouldn't be easy and would change day by day. Just another hurdle. In my opinion we are in the home stretch here. Layla will keep improving and be ready to go home soon. Jeremiah and I will divide and conquer what needs to be done for the girls along with our tribe of people willing to help. So many things have worked out already, and this won't be any different. I usually post about Layla, and she's still doing amazing things. But so much work had to go into Cali, too, so I thought I should share the beautiful memories she made with the family who loved on her so I could be with Layla. Pretty amazing summer so far, and I am so grateful.

Day 36: Sunday, June 26th

As fate would have it, I woke up sick. I felt it coming the night before. My throat was on fire, and my ears were throbbing. There was no way I was going to pass this to Layla. This would be the first day I would spend away from her. It was almost perfect though; it was the last day I had with Cali.

Layla: Am I dead?

Me: No baby, you are alive and getting better.

Layla: Am I alone?

Me: No baby, you are never alone. Daddy is with you.

Layla: What do I have to do?

Me: You just have to keep getting better. You're doing so good.

Layla: Why did we have to do this?

Me: You were in a bad accident baby. We have to fix your body, and then we can go home.

Layla: What do I have to do?

160

Me: You have to learn a few more things. It won't be long.

Layla: How long?

Me: Few more weeks

Layla: How long?

Me: It depends on what the doctors say.

Layla: Time feels like it's going in circles.

Me: I know, baby.

Layla: Why are my legs unshaved?

Me: You've been in the hospital for a while. Do you want Mommy to shave them?

Layla: Yes. When do I get out?

Me: Soon baby

Layla: Am I alive?

Me: Yes, you are. You have an injury. Every day will get easier.

Layla: Promise?

Me: Yes, I promise.

Texts like this trickled in through the day. She was determined to get some answers. It reminded me of Layla before. When Layla wanted answers, she was relentless. This Layla was fragile, but her spirit was still there. The doctors warned us she wouldn't be the same. No one really explained it well. It seemed like there were a ton of possibilities. I knew from research: No one came back the same. The person you knew would be a different person. It's a very strange feeling. It looks like your person, but it's definitely not your person. It's almost cruel. You miss them. It's like they are being dangled in front of you, but the parts that made them, them, are gone. I knew it was still too early to tell, but the fear sits in the back of your mind. It waits for any opportunity to overtake you. There's a reason the Bible says, "Do not be afraid," 365 times. Fear is powerful.

Jessica and Mack stopped by Bethany's to bring us lunch. In some ways, it was a goodbye. Cali was leaving, and I was checking in to Layla's room. That day, though, I was excited to meet their new addition. After they adopted Charlie, they got pregnant through IVF and welcomed Chancy to the family. Jessica and Mack made parenting look easy, and I loved being able to witness it. I loved that they had been blessed with this perfect little family. Looking in, you'd never know what they went through to get there. I knew, and it made me happy to see it end up like this.

Our families always blended well, mostly because we shared the same sense of humor. Mack and Jeremiah could have been brothers the way they interacted. They could bounce jokes off each other for hours. It was fun to be around. We made light of bad haircuts or bad situations. None of us were easily offended. Laughing at your situation helps sometimes. While we were sitting at the table, Mack got a text.

"Jeremiah just asked me if he was alive?" he said puzzled.

We all burst into laughter when I explained Layla's new texting skills.

For my last day with Cali, we went to a special dinner together. We avoided talking about her departure the next day; we just tried staying in the moment and being silly. I was rarely apart from Cali. She had been attached to my hip since birth. In some ways, I thought it might be good for her. It would give her a chance to bond with her dad. It was going to

162

hurt, though, and I knew that. We finished dinner and ran by the puppy store for one last visit with our puppy friends. I was still getting multiple texts from Layla, so I suggested Cali try texting her. I was originally worried Layla's state might scare Cali, but it ended up being a great idea. Cali was amused by Layla's responses, and Layla was more engaged with her than she typically would have been. I wondered if this experience was going to create a special bond between them, too.

Before bed, I checked in with Jeremiah. I knew this was not going to be easy for any of us. We started with a FaceTime call, and during it, Layla gave me and Cali the finger. Like, she flipped us off! It was very unlike her and surprised us all. The part we loved was her smirk after she did it. She was trying to be funny. She knew this was not an acceptable gesture, but we couldn't help but laugh. There were glimpses of her old self that came more often now. As much as I didn't want her flipping people off, it showed cognitively she knew how to get a rise out of us. And of course, she knew she wouldn't get in trouble.

Me: You have done such an amazing job with Layla. Please give our Cali the same Daddy love. She's going to need it.

Jeremiah: Oh, I have big plans for Ms. Cali.

Me: Thank you, it makes my heart so happy.

Jeremiah: This is my last night; this is really tough for me to leave her.

Me: I know. You did so good though, better than I could have ever done. Now you are needed for another role, a very important one.

Jeremiah: We had some scary nights on cooling blankets, buried in ice, with machines beeping and buzzing, and the sound of the vent sawing away in the background. Then we had some beautiful mornings just waking up to see her still fighting.

163

Me: Amen. We will never forget it, and we came out stronger each day.

Jeremiah: I'm sitting here crying, watching her sleep so quietly now.

Me: You did good baby, so good.

Jeremiah: I don't think I ever really stopped to think about everything, just pushed forward.

Me: There was no time to think, or plan, just go.

Jeremiah: I just want her to know I am sorry for every time I said, "We'll do it tomorrow," or "I'm tired today, Lay," or all the times she asked to go to the beach to go surfing and I said I had work to do.

Me: You can't do that to yourself. You are a great dad. We can ALL improve, and I love you. Thank you for everything.

Jeremiah: Love you most.

I went to bed last night not feeling 100% and woke up pretty much the same. To be safe, I didn't see Layla today, but she was in good hands, as usual, with Jeremiah. Getting her sick means something much different now. Her new texting skills are both good and bad. You can see she's still very confused. You get a good look at what's going on in her head, and it's not easy to see her going through that, but it's also amazing how well she articulates it. Plus, you get occasional glimpses of Layla with her teenager slang mixed in. She went on a texting spree today, and a handful of you received texts. Pretty sure she asked everyone when she can go home, and we just need to reassure her she's safe and healing. As confused as she is, she was aware I wasn't there. I think she sent me 147 texts asking where I was and when I was coming back, followed by texts making me promise not to leave again. She didn't get to visit Cali today, but

164

they were able to text, and Layla got a ton of belly laughs out of Cali. I actually think this worked out better and will be something they can use in the weeks going forward. Plus, Cali felt very useful helping answer the plethora of questions Layla had. Tomorrow starts a new chapter for our family's story, and I have peace about it. Another lesson we will gain from this to give us a whole new appreciation for having each other daily. We've had to all adapt daily to some crazy stuff, and we are still smiling, our family is still whole, and that little girl is alive against the odds. So many miracles.

Day 37: Monday, June 27th

Layla: Are you coming?

Me: Yes baby, and I'm never leaving again. I need you to do good at therapy first, OK?

Layla: When are you coming?

Me: 1 o'clock. I need you to do therapy first, then I will be there after.

Layla: How long will you stay?

Me: Forever. I won't have to leave again.

Layla: I feel like the days go in circles.

Me: I know baby. It's going to get easier, I promise.

Layla: It's going in circles.

Me: Your body is healing. It will get better.

Layla: Are you coming?

Me: Yes, after therapy.

Layla: Promise?

Me: Yes, I promise.

Layla: Promise?

Me: Do you trust Mommy?

Layla: Yes.

Me: I promise you it's going to be OK, and you are safe.

Layla: You promise you are coming?

Me: Yes, I promise, and I won't leave again.

Layla: OK

Me: Everything is going to be OK, Layla.

Layla: You won't leave again?

Me: Never ever, from today on.

Her texts shook my soul when they arrived at 7:00 am that morning. They physically hurt. I hated the fear in her words. It was everything I imagined she would have said the day of the accident if she could've said it. She was scared and needed me. She was also confused. She forgot who Jeremiah was for an entire day. That one stung. All these things were to be expected but didn't make it any easier. We wanted to know how this ended. What was Layla going to be like when it was all said and done?

Cali and I went to breakfast at the same place we went when we first arrived here. We pretended like it was our tradition, even though we'd only been there once before. Then we walked next door and played with the puppies again. They even recognized us, so maybe that was more of our tradition. We stopped at a store so Cali could get Layla a teddy bear. She wanted to leave a piece of her with her sister. Then we headed into the city. When we arrived, Layla was in therapy, so Jeremiah had a few minutes to spend with us in the garage before Mary Jane and Kerry arrived to take him to the airport. It did not feel like enough time.

This was goodbye for a while.

I think it hit all of us at once. My heart ached as Cali clung to me sobbing. I wanted to tell her I was sorry for this. I hated that in order to help one daughter, I had to hurt the other. I knew we were doing the right thing; it was just going to take time to see that. I kissed them goodbye and watched them drive away, taking a piece of me with them.

Mary Jane stayed back with me. Kerry would pick her up later. I was going to show her around my new home and let her visit with Layla. Last time she saw her, Layla was still unconscious. As we were approaching Layla's door, she was passing us in her wheelchair heading to her next therapy. She suddenly extended her arm, signaling she wanted us to hug her. We played along and acted like this was normal behavior, but it was not. Layla had never done anything like that before. We kissed her goodbye and finished the walk to her room in shock. Once inside, we turned to each other with tears in our eyes and celebrated those hugs.

I settled myself in to my new home. It wasn't as scary as I expected. I felt like a mom on a mission. I was actually looking forward to this. There was something comforting about being with her and not having to leave. It was difficult always switching gears between the two girls and sleeping in two places. This felt more stable to me, like I could get more done being in one place. I love schedules and routines, and there was plenty of that here. I was almost built for this.

Tomorrow, Layla would be having the wires removed from her jaw. The surgery would take a couple hours, and I was allowed to accompany her. The surgery would take place next door at the Piedmont Hospital. I explained it to Layla, but she didn't seem very interested. Her focus was the phone. She randomly FaceTimed a few people and sent a few more texts. Her main focus seemed to switch from texting me to texting Cali.

Mary Jane brought me a book I could read to Layla—something else to help distract her. Layla and I shared a love of reading, more so when she was younger. I often had my nose in a book, and she mimicked this at an early age. She picked up reading quickly, and once she could, she took over the bedtime reading. It was another season of her life that I now felt I didn't get enough time in. One day she was reading children's books, then overnight it became chapter books. It gave a new meaning to the expression, "Don't blink."

Day 38: Tuesday, June 28th

Whenever Layla had surgery scheduled, they would cut her medications off. One of those medications was blood thinners—the injection she got in her stomach at night. This is also the reason I wasn't allowed to shave her legs. Since her surgery was today, she didn't get the blood thinner the night before, so I was allowed to give her a shower and finally shave her legs the next morning.

When Layla was in middle school, she started bugging me about shaving her legs. Arguing with her was pointless sometimes; she would beat us with persistence. I finally agreed, but I was at work at the time and promised her we would do it together when I got home. I thought it would be a chance to bond. When I walked in the door, Layla appeared with cuts and Band-Aids all over her freshly shaven legs. She clearly thought she didn't need my help. Well, she needed my help this time. This was the moment she stole from me many years ago. It didn't look like I had pictured, but I was still getting a chance to help her. I positioned her wheelchair facing the shower and covered her trach, just like I was trained. Then I crawled around the shower floor, getting splashed by water as I shaved her legs for the first time. This was another one of those situations where I was laughing at myself. When I looked up at Layla, she had that same smirk from the other day. Obviously, she also saw the humor in this.

"Well, I got to shave your legs after all," I teased.

The nurses came for Layla around 10:00. They brought in a bed to transport her and asked Layla to scoot over into it. Layla proceeded to steamroll herself there instead and had the whole team laughing. As they wheeled her out, I was excited to see the secret tunnel to the hospital at last. We took the elevator to the basement and maneuvered our way down a few hallways. The secret tunnel was not what I expected. It was bright and colorful with pretty artwork on the walls. It was more like a happy tunnel. It didn't feel like a hospital anymore. I liked it down there.

When we entered Piedmont, that changed. This felt very much like a hospital—a big one. Our nurse tucked us into one of the little bays. There were a lot of those here. Everyone was waiting for some type of procedure. There were no doors to our space, only a curtain, so we could hear everything going on around us. I could hear a nearby ventilator. I hadn't heard this sound in a long time. My heart sped up immediately. It felt like it was beating through my chest, and there was a ringing in my ears. Panic attacks had become a regular thing for me, but this was no time for a panic attack. I tried to only focus on Layla and just breathe. Layla had a different look in her eyes, almost frightened. Could she possibly know what was going on? Typically, she sat through most procedures without any reaction. We were holding hands when I asked her if she was okay, and she began shaking her head no. She was scared! It's not that I wanted her to be, but this was more of an expected reaction. Eventually, she had me crawl into her stretcher with her so we could communicate on the phone. She was nervous about this. She was afraid she would feel something. I kept explaining she would be asleep, but that wasn't enough for her. Her concern was waking up during it.

This felt a lot like Layla.

We had no set surgery time, so we just had to wait until the surgeon could get to us. We sat in that little bay until 2:00 pm. Most of that time was spent with me reassuring her everything was going to be okay. When they finally took her back, I headed to the waiting area. It was going to be a few hours. We had been at this since 10:00 am, but I was too afraid to go far, even if I was starving. I found a little coffee kiosk and tucked myself into one of the waiting room chairs. Two hours later, they called my name, then moved me to another waiting room. The doctor came in and briefed me on how well it went. He also put a few stitches in the stoma since it kept opening larger. One of the nurses took me to Layla so we could head back. I could finally exhale seeing her little face. She was definitely in pain, but she was done. I was excited to get back to our room. She gave me a thumbs up and off we went.

I was happy to be back in our space again. The day had been very long. I was excited for Layla to be able to open her mouth again, too. I hoped it would help her find her voice. She was extremely fatigued when we got back, so the remainder of the day would be spent resting. I handed her the phone and asked how she was feeling.

"Can I talk yet?" she asked.

How I wished it were that easy.

I started sorting through her mail. This girl would get dozens of cards and packages from her supporters, and it was always fun going through them. My cousin had sent her a sign that read, "She is strong." It was from Proverbs, and it was perfect. It was the same verse printed on the pink shirts everyone was now wearing for Layla. We loved seeing those shirts being worn all over. I hung up her sign nearby her bed so everyone who entered knew.

"She is strong."

I remembered when the doctors gave us her initial prognosis. We knew there was a possibility they were wrong. If anyone could do it, it would be Layla. Like the sign said, she was strong. We tried telling them then. With tears in his eyes Jeremiah told them, "You don't know this girl." Thank God he was right!

172

Her nurse came in and informed me that Thursday I would be meeting with the doctor for her assessment. He was going to go over what they expected for Layla at the end of this and share a percentage of how much we could expect back. I didn't even know this was happening until then. Now, I was worried. This was something better fit for Jeremiah. I had sworn off listening to negative opinions to the point I typically left whenever a doctor started talking about the things Layla would "never" do. Now I had to be trapped in a room with this guy telling me how bad this was going to end. Why couldn't he just send an email or something? I did not want to attend this meeting, especially alone.

Me: I'm scared.

Jeremiah: Why?

Me: The thing about her not recognizing you and the nurse saying the brain cells never come back. I'm really scared of what the doctor is going to say at this meeting.

Jeremiah: OK, those are legitimate worries. But her recognition is getting better as she heals.

Me: Nurse said the doctor will base assessment off her injury and other patients with the same one and how they turned out. I know from reading how this typically turns out, and I don't want to hear it.

Jeremiah: Yes, but the doctors in ICU were wrong about all kinds of stuff too.

Me: I'm scared he's gonna send me into a spiral. I wish you were here.

Jeremiah: You have to remember who got her this far.

Me: I know, but you are scared, too. I saw it in your face.

Jeremiah: What do you mean?

173

Me: You were saying she had damage to section of the brain that affects her personality.

Jeremiah: Doctors said that, but they've been wrong about everything so far.

Me: What if this doctor says bad stuff?

Jeremiah: He won't be the first to say bad stuff Ali. He won't be the first to say what science said her future will be, and she's proven everyone wrong so far.

Me: What if he's a know it all?

Jeremiah: He's looking at a girl that even nurses said progressed faster than anyone they've ever seen.

Me: I just don't want to hear bad stuff.

Jeremiah: No matter what he says, if anyone can overcome this it's her. She's special Ali, we always knew that!
They told us she wouldn't survive, she did.
Said she wouldn't move, she did.
Said she wouldn't breathe, she did.
Said she wouldn't walk, she did.
When she smiled after giving you the finger, I knew she was in there.

Me: That was pretty funny.

Jeremiah: She has a long road ahead, and it's going to be a lot of work, but she can do this.

Me: OK I trust you. I'm sorry, I just needed to process that out loud for a moment.

Jeremiah: That's OK, it's how I do it, too. Remember where we started, be grateful where we are, and faithful where we are headed.

There he went again knowing exactly what to say. Plus, he wasn't going to make me handle the meeting alone. The plan was to do a conference call so at least one of us would retain the information. He promised me I wouldn't have to speak if I didn't want to. Plugging my ears was even an option if it got too intense. I sent out a call for prayer to my inner circle. I was going to need it to get through that meeting without a meltdown. I don't know why I cared so much about what doctors said. I knew they had been wrong so far. I had faith she was going to conquer this. I'd just rather not hear their doubts because, for a moment, they would become mine. I knew they had to prepare you, but I don't operate that way. I'd rather stay hopeful till it's over. I wanted to hear what's possible, not likely.

All I needed was a little hope.

Day 39: Wednesday, June 29th

The morning started busy. She woke up with less pain than the day before and had therapies scheduled from 8:00 am to 1:00 pm with a few breaks scattered in. They were going to give her the swallow test and see if she was able to chew. They started with juice and water, and she was able to handle both. I imagined it felt so good to finally have a sip of water. The only liquid she had up until then was the water from brushing her teeth. Next, they tried yogurt. Once again, Layla handled it well. The final test would be chewing. Pancakes were on the menu for today. Shepherd was known for their pancakes, but the old Layla did not like pancakes. When they tried it, she didn't even attempt to chew them. She just spit them right out. It was hard to tell if this was because of jaw pain or Layla being picky (though my guess was Layla being picky). She had always been difficult to feed and so stubborn about things she didn't want to eat. Finally, they gave up on chewing and decided to move on to speaking.

It had been over a week trying to get her to speak, and it was disheartening each day she couldn't do it. We missed her voice. There were several variables that could be causing it—the worst one being she damaged her vocal cords from the intubation. She would mouth the words, but no sound came out of her. Once again, I returned to the room with my silent daughter. I didn't want it to get me down, so I pulled out some crosswords and word searches to keep us distracted. She didn't particularly like doing them, but she liked me confined to the bed with her, so she would play along if I stayed.

The respiratory team usually came in every few hours to clean her trach and change the bandages. It was not my favorite thing to see. Usually, I avoided looking all together. Around 5:00 that day, a nurse came in for her trach care. It seemed routine at first. I was laying in the bed with her when the woman asked me for help. I really didn't want to help with this, but before I could refuse, she was pulling the entire trach out and cleaning the area. I had never seen them do this before; this did not seem routine at all. She asked me to hold a cloth over the hole in Layla's neck while she grabbed another piece of equipment. My head was spinning. This was way more up close and personal than I ever got with the trach. She inserted another tube into the hole and got her put back together while I sat there wide eyed.

Casually, the nurse said to Layla, "Say hi to Mommy."

Before I could even register what was happening, the tiniest whisper came from Layla's mouth.

"HI, Mommy."

I was not prepared for this, and I definitely was not expecting it. I could barely get the words out to thank the woman; all I could do was sob. Layla could speak. It was only a whisper, but it was the greatest sound I ever heard. Right then, I wanted to fall on my knees and thank God. How did we ever deserve this gift? How did we get this far? How is it possible this girl had her voice again? I grabbed my phone and FaceTimed Jeremiah and Cali. Then, the tears started all over.

Day 40: Thursday, June 30th

Every night I slept right next to Layla in the chair thing. Every morning around 6:30, I would see her little hand reach over the side, waiting for me to take it. It's the best part of the day. Today that hand came with a bonus greeting.

"Good morning, Mommy," she whispered.

She was also all smiles today, which just made my day. That made everything easier. The therapists even noticed the shift in her attitude. She seemed happier, a lot happier, and I was so grateful.

She left for speech around 9:00 and was expected back about 11:30. I had my meeting with the doctor scheduled during her time away. I armed myself with God's Word going into it. I pulled out every verse I could find about being strong. I prayed with as many people as I could and spiritually prepared myself for the things this man was going to say. My hands were sweating, and I felt nauseous, but I was ready. Finally, the case manager came to get me. I took a few deep breaths and followed her out the door.

She led me to a conference room with a large table. Layla's doctor was sitting at the head, with six empty chairs on both sides of him. I contemplated sitting far away from him so I could tune him out if I needed. On the opposite wall was a flatscreen TV with images of a brain—Layla's brain. The case manager sat across from me with a speaker phone in the center. Jeremiah was linked into that little box. I was already choking back tears. I wanted to tell them my husband would get them if they made me cry, but I knew the little box didn't quite have same effect as seeing him in person. All doctors ever did was tell me bad news, so I expected no different from this one.

He wasted no time getting into the severity of her injury. I'd heard all this before. I understood about half of it. I wanted to stop him and tell him to get to the end already. He started going over each brain bleed Layla had. I knew there were many, and this was going to take a while. He highlighted her largest bleed and started explaining the significance of this one. If it was a millimeter to the right, she would have been instantly paralyzed at best. I had never heard that detail before. I liked learning that. It was just more proof of Layla's miracle—another one of those lucky coincidences. He shifted into the brain shearing and the damage to her brain stem. He made some comments about how bad the impact must have been to have shearing this extensive. He almost seemed impressed by it. He then pulled up the images of her broken jaw. I had never seen these before either. I couldn't help my mouth from falling open. I had no idea how bad she had broken it. Her jaw looked cut in two with the broken piece angling toward the center of her mouth. It was probably a good thing I had never seen this scan before. It was intense.

Finally, he started his closing statements. I knew it was coming. He was going to tell me all the things my daughter would never do. I braced myself and started taking a few deep breaths, internally repeating all the encouragement people had given me. I was partially tuning him out, but I swear I heard him say something about full recovery. I stopped him right there.

"Wait, what!?" I asked.

He seemed confused before he repeated himself.

"Given Layla's progress, I expect her to make a full recovery," he assured us once more.

Why didn't he lead with this?! Why did he have to start with all that doom and gloom? I was sitting there stunned. When I could finally speak, I was fumbling over my words. I had so many questions. He understood my confusion; without saying the word itself, he told us what we'd been praying for: She was a miracle.

He explained that Layla's brain was finding new pathways for her body to function again and doing it exceptionally well. It was happening fast, much faster than they'd anticipated. I instantly felt bad for wanting to kick him under the table for seeming to doubt her earlier. I wanted to hug him, but he didn't seem like the hugging type. He ended by giving us a discharge date of August 3rd. Finally, a doctor with good news!

Full recovery…

This meant Layla was expected to eventually lead a normal life. She would possibly have some challenges but not the kind we expected at the beginning. Plus, we like a good challenge! It was the first time we had an accurate idea of how this would end. It made things so much easier knowing that information. It was going to be a lot of time, work, and patience, but we would get our daughter back eventually.

Layla was expected back at 11:30. Right around 11:15 the door swung open and in rolled Layla, alone. I waited, assuming the therapists were catching up soon, but no one came. I asked Layla if she had come back by herself, and she shook her head yes. I asked if she was allowed to do that, and she shook her head no. I had to laugh, which made her smile. I wheeled her back to the gym so she could fess up to her big escape. Apparently, it was free time, and Layla decided she would rather have free time with me. We were all laughing at her spirit. The distance she traveled by memory was quite impressive. When Layla wanted to do something, she found a way. Just like her brain was doing finding new pathways, she found her way back to me.

Day 41: Friday, July 1st

If I had to leave Layla unattended, I had to put the lap belt on her. It was a white belt that kept her secured to the bed and could only be opened with a nurse's key. She hated it, but we couldn't risk her potentially hurting herself with a fall. She had never attempted getting out of bed unassisted before, but she also changed by the hour. A bad fall could mean starting all over. So, each morning, I would secure the belt and run down the hall to get coffee. I always explained what I was doing, so she knew I'd be back in five minutes. Today, when I explained, she whispered that she wanted to come. I was surprised. Typically, Layla did not volunteer to get out of bed until she had to. Getting her out of bed was a process. I had to dress her and help her into her wheelchair, then secure her in. It added about 15 minutes to my coffee run, but I enjoyed the idea of having her with me. I rolled her down the hall and sent Jeremiah a quick video of my new coffee buddy.

Jeremiah: Good morning, sorry you have to drink crappy coffee.

Me: I don't mind the crappy coffee when she's with me.

Since she was up, I brought her along while I did laundry, too. The nurses seemed happy to see us together, up and about so early. I was getting good at managing her care. I rarely needed the nursing staff for anything except medications and unlocking that belt. They often insisted on helping, but I enjoyed this. I liked knowing I could do it. I was grateful for them teaching me, but I wanted their time to be spent with someone who didn't have a family member there to help. I was also learning how much nurses do. It takes a special person to care for a stranger like they do.

Today, Jen was going to attempt to get Layla to chew again. I encouraged Layla to cooperate so she could start eating real foods instead of using the feeding tube. I wanted to start putting weight back on her. She had lost 25 pounds since this started, and she was already too skinny to begin with. I couldn't believe she even had 25 pounds to lose! This time, Jen tried a chocolate chip cookie. We needed her to eat and pass the test before the weekend started or she would be restricted to the feeding tube only until Monday. Thankfully, Layla nibbled enough cookie for Jen to clear her for puree type foods over the weekend.

Layla had always been a sugar kid, so much so that I often found a candy stash in her room. It was another battle I had with her often. The sugar addiction didn't fit the way she preferred to eat though. She had expensive tastes. She rarely ordered off a kid's menu and preferred filet mignon or some type of seafood. But every meal was finished off with ice cream or some type of sweet. She always wanted the good stuff! When Jen returned her to the room, the pressure was on. What was I going to give this girl for her first liquid meal? I ran through a list of options for Layla. She decided on an Oreo milkshake from Shake Shack and sucked it down. The joy was short lived; soon after, she started asking for food. I was going to have to get real creative with protein shakes because we were a long way from Monday.

The more aware she becomes, the more she misses home and asks why we can't go. It's a little heartbreaking, and she forgets a lot, so I repeatedly must tell her the story of her miracle. Sometimes she cries, or hugs me, or thanks everyone who's been with us. Sometimes she seems lost in the story and sometimes has a lot of questions. Emotions are a good sign. I joke with her and tell her we are just 2 chicks living in our Atlanta condo with room service and a doorman. She smiles when I say it. There's a lot of things we've had to learn to do for her while she can't. I know I'm supposed to see this as sad, and don't get me wrong, it's a lot of work. But I also see it as a privilege. I love my kids immensely, as I'm sure most parents do. The minute you meet them you are staring at something you love 10 times more than yourself. That love doesn't always translate to teenagers because they are, well, teenagers. We got the opportunity to show her how much we'd do and how far we'd go because of that love. That just seems pretty awesome to me. Speaking of awesome, I got to order her a milkshake today! She is allowed purée type foods, so I let her pick. Tomorrow we will try a smoothie.

Day 42: Saturday, July 2nd

Layla's weeks were typically jam packed with therapies and activities. It would wear her out, so we rarely had time or energy to do things she chose. That was my favorite part of the weekends. It was quieter, and we had a lot more free time. In some ways, we were getting to know each other again, and weekends were perfect for this. She joined me for my coffee run again before she had a few brief therapies and was done before lunch.

The day was ours.

The first thing she wanted was Starbucks. It had always been a favorite of hers, and I was excited to see her enjoy it again. I handed her the app to place the order, curious if she'd remember what she used to get. Her drink order was a mile long, but she remembered it. She amazed me with the strange things she could recollect. She couldn't remember really big things, like getting her driver's license. I even showed her the ID card, but she had no memory of it ever happening. I wondered how many family memories were lost, or if she would eventually get them back. I knew her short-term memory was struggling, but those were long-term memories. All those special moments we worked so hard to give her could possibly be gone. It was a thought we tried not thinking about. I just tried to remember that she still had a lot of healing to do.

Today I was going to take her on an unassisted walk. The unassisted part was mostly for me, not her. I was cleared to walk alone with her, but we didn't have time before today to attempt it. Today, we were restricted to the second floor of the hospital because of the trach and respiratory cart that followed. We returned to the same hallway she first walked, and I talked us through the steps. We successfully made it down the hall to the window. She was chatty and had a lot of questions, mostly about going home. She also was determined to get food, specifically Chick-fil-a nuggets. She stopped several people in the hall asking if they had nuggets, as if they carried them in their pockets or something. I finally pacified her by ordering another milkshake and returning to the room.

Usually, Layla headed straight for the bed. Today she wanted to walk around her room and examine the pictures and cards that were wallpapering the space. It was the first time she seemed to notice them. She picked up each photograph and card to carefully study them. It took an hour to make it halfway through the room.

Then, she broke down in tears.

Other than the first day, I had not seen Layla's tears. She was crying so hard that she could barely get the words out to tell me the pictures made her sad because life wasn't like that anymore. I scrambled for the right words to comfort her, but instead, I ended up crying with her. She was right, life was different now. I missed it, too. I couldn't promise her it would ever be the same again, but I knew we would be okay. We would find our groove and a new sense of normal. I wanted her to know it was okay to grieve that, just like Corrie had told me. So, we had a good, messy cry over milkshakes.

After our breakdown, I thought it was a good time to FaceTime Cali. Cali could bring Layla peace like no one else. Layla didn't challenge her answers like she did with me. Cali was so patient with her. In many ways, it was like their roles reversed, and Cali had become the big sister. Watching them was something straight out of Hallmark movie. Cali would give her tours of our home and show her the dogs. She used such tenderness when Layla would start up again about wanting to come home. She played games with her for hours and never turned down the calls. Layla didn't converse much, but Cali found ways to fill the silence. She had the wisdom to save her questions about Layla's mental state for times I was alone. I knew how much she hurt seeing her sister suffer, but she put on a good face to protect Layla. I often wondered if the role was too big for her, but in many ways, she was built for it. Her only wish was to get her sister home and our family back together.

Day 43: Sunday, July 3rd

Something seemed to ignite in Layla over the weekend. She seemed determined, like the little girl I saw fall on her face 100 times trying to perfect a tumble routine. Usually, I had to persuade her into walking practice or pushing her own wheelchair. Today she initiated two separate walks and maneuvered her chair on her own all the way there. It was like her rest was done, and she was ready for the next steps.

Kerry stopped by for a visit. He was easy to hang out with, and he didn't mind Layla's silence. Sometimes it felt like she wasn't paying attention to us, especially when she was absorbed in a video game with Cali. On one of the walls hung a large pink sign someone had sent us. It read, "You are braver than you believe, stronger than you seem, and smarter than you think." The sign had been hung there for weeks. Kerry, making conversation, asked Layla if she liked that decoration. Without even looking up, she mumbled, "Missing an R." We both were confused, and I thought maybe she was rambling nonsense. Her speech was also difficult to understand sometimes, so I asked her to repeat what she said.

She finally looked up at me, unamused, and boldly repeated, "Stronger is missing an R."

Layla had always been the spelling police. Kerry and I looked up at the banner. She was right; the word stronger had an R missing. No one had even noticed it before. We both laughed, and I teased that Layla was faking this whole thing.

Twice a day I would read a devotional to Layla. She seemed to enjoy it. Just like she did as a child, she asked me if, instead, she could read it out loud today. I figured it was good exercise for her brain and her voice, so I willingly gave it up. She wanted to read Kerry that day's devotional. There was something so sweet about listening to her read. Her voice was soft and whispery, and she didn't know when to pause for breath. It was almost childlike. When she was finished performing, Kerry asked if she wanted to recite his favorite verse from the bible. He began reciting the 23rd Psalm. After each line, he would pause and patiently wait for Layla to mimic his words.

The LORD is my shepherd; I shall not want.
He maketh me to lie down in green pastures: he leadeth me beside the still waters.
He restoreth my soul: he leadeth me in the paths of righteousness for his name's sake.
Yea, though I walk through the valley of the shadow of death, I will fear no evil: for thou art with me;
thy rod and thy staff they comfort me.
Thou preparest a table before me in the presence of mine enemies: thou anointest my head with oil; my cup runneth over.
Surely goodness and mercy shall follow me all the days of my life: and I will dwell in the house of the LORD forever.

By the end, Kerry and I were fighting back tears. There was something emotional about listening to those words coming out of her mouth. I had only ever heard that Scripture used for funerals, so I had associated it with death. I never really thought about the context. This was not a sad passage after all. This was about hope and comfort. No wonder they use it at funerals! This passage acknowledged we all have pain and suffering, but God would be with us in it. Like a shepherd, He would protect us, just like He had done with Layla. It almost seemed ironic I was at a place called Shepherd Center. God led us here and cleared the path, placing the right people in our way. His hand was in this from the beginning, and we were never alone.

Day 44: Monday, July 4th

I couldn't imagine spending a major holiday in the hospital. Christmas, for example, seems like it would be tough to be stuck in a hospital. I spent two birthdays in the hospital with the birth of my daughters, but you can postpone a birthday party. You can't really postpone a holiday.

Today was the 4th of July, and we would be spending it at Shepherd. I guess out of all the holidays, this would be the easiest one to get over. Usually we went to the beach or had a party, and I always coordinated outfits. I liked any opportunity to dress up and take pictures. The good part was, Shepherd provided us with shirts. The bad part was, we were stuck in the room. Mary Jane and Kerry stopped by for a visit and brought us food. Mary Jane had decorated the room and brought festive headbands for us to wear. I figured we could watch fireworks from her window later and make the best of it.

The hospital had a different feeling that day. Everyone seemed to be in celebration mode. It was calmer, like a Saturday. Layla was having another one of those happy days, and I secretly wished this happy version of her would stick around. She had more testing for her eating happening that afternoon. They were trying to get her a bigger menu to choose from or, at the least, the nuggets she was still talking about. She was so focused on asking Jen over the weekend, she even asked me to write it down so she wouldn't forget. After therapy, she rolled back into the room with a

190

bag of Fruit Loops she was cramming into her mouth. There would be no nuggets today, but she was allowed to eat some solid foods. It was a compromise, but it still didn't stop her from asking 100 more times.

Tomorrow would be my son's birthday. I had always spent his birthday with him. I liked making a big deal about birthdays. I knew this year would be difficult because he had moved out, but this was a different level of difficult. He never wanted a big event, usually just a family party and home cooking. He was easily pleased and mostly just wanted time together.

Jeremiah Jr: It will be my first birthday without y'all.

Me: I know, I miss you so much it stings. If it makes you feel better, I'm spending the Fourth of July in a hospital.

Jeremiah Jr: Just like 20 years ago.

Me: YES! True. Listening to fireworks in a hospital.

Jeremiah Jr: Kinda cool then. Different situation but similar at the same time.

Me: It is. Thank you for changing my perspective. Wise beyond your years Jeremiah.

> *The Peachtree Road Race was today. It's a big thing in Atlanta, and the runners go right by Shepherd. There's a whole wheelchair division, which is amazing to me. They allow some of the patients to go out and watch and cheer. Layla and I watched from the window and talked about next year getting to come back and check it out from a different angle. She had a few therapy sessions and returned to me with a bag of Fruit Loops she was very happily eating. She was cleared to eat some more foods today. She's still asking for nuggets, which she can't have, but she comprised with Starbucks egg bites and a cake pop, plus one of her nurses brought her that drink she likes. I've*

said it before, but this place is special. You feel it when you walk down the halls. You see it with the interactions of patients with staff. You watch strangers care for your loved one like they were their own, and it's indescribable. They also have cool shirts. Since we got here, I can't stop complimenting the shirts. There's all different ones the staff wear, and I love them. I was really excited when someone came to deliver two T-shirts to me and Layla for the 4th of July, probably more excited than I should have been. I also got to twin with my girl (plus the majority of the hospital.) My aunt and uncle visited today and brought us dinner. Layla got mac and cheese, which she settled for after getting denied the nuggets once again. We couldn't see any fireworks from the window, so we settled for watching everyone's posts and a FaceTime with Cali. Happy 4th everyone!

Day 45: Tuesday, July 5th

I had told Layla the therapists were the keys to her going home. It meant she had to cooperate and do what was asked of her. Since I had told her that, she seemed to approach therapy differently. She was much happier about going and had a better attitude with them. Layla was always easy to coach, but only if she wanted to be doing it. Her cheerleading coaches always complimented how well she took directions. She's had a lot of great coaches over the years, but there was one she was most fond of: Coach T. I used to tell him he spoke Layla. If she had a hard day at school, she would tell T. If she was struggling with a stunt, she wanted T's help. When she wanted to learn a new skill, T was the guy for the job. They were very close.

The day of her tracheotomy surgery, T passed away unexpectedly. I didn't have the heart to tell her, and I hoped it would be a while before she found out. That morning, while scrolling through Instagram, she saw it. Her little face turned to me, concerned as she asked, "Did coach T die?"

I watched her trying to process all the emotions that came with that news. I once again fumbled for the right things to say to make it better. I gave her all the details I knew and reminded her how much he loved her. Sometimes, you just have to cry it out.

When the therapy team arrived that day, they pulled me aside. They planned on surprising Layla with the nuggets she had been asking for. The timing couldn't have been more perfect, so I ordered as many nuggets as a mobile order would allow. It was a bit excessive, but it felt like a celebration that I knew she'd want to share with everyone. Layla would be eating in the gym today, and there were always other patients around. That meant plenty of people to share with. Still, we had to slow her down from inhaling them all! They had to be cut into pieces, but she said it was the best thing ever. She even got to meet the man that screamed at night sometimes and share some with him. It made him a lot less scary to put a face to the voice. He politely thanked her; it was nice to see him this way.

I was starting to understand why someone would choose to work with brain injury. The people were all so vulnerable. They were all learning from scratch, and the therapists get to be a part of that. They got to help them find their way home. In many ways, it was beautiful.

Just like the nuggets, Layla had been nagging Jen about removing her trach. This had become a daily thing. Layla's trach was capped off, so it wasn't doing anything. It was basically on standby in case it was needed. Typically, they leave it this way for a few weeks, and Layla was only on day five. This was explained repeatedly to her, but she wasn't letting it go. Clearly, they didn't realize that, even with a brain injury, she would be persistent. She asked a few more times on the walk back to the room until Jen finally said, "I'll see what I can do."

I assumed Jen was just trying to pacify her so she'd stop asking. An hour later a doctor walked into the room and asked if she wanted the trach removed. I thought it more of a rhetorical question, but I played along.

"Yes," I answered. "What day?"

He looked at us and said, "How about now?"

He wasn't kidding. He was going to remove it right then and there at her bedside. All the fuss that goes into getting it, and he removed it in under a minute. It was like pulling out a splinter. He bandaged her up and left the room. Just like the day she spoke, I wasn't prepared for it, but I liked these kinds of surprises. It was another step closer to getting us home.

With the trach gone, it meant we didn't need the respiratory cart that followed Layla everywhere she went. It also meant I could take her to other parts of the hospital. No more being confined to the second floor! We just gained a lot more room to run. If I could take her with me, I wouldn't have to put the bed restraints on each time I left. It's not that I left often, but occasionally, I had to eat or take showers. With the trach removed, it just felt like freedom, even if we were still confined to Shepherd. She had taken so many big steps today; we were miles ahead of where we started.

We had a new nurse that night. She had heard the rumors about Layla and was looking forward to meeting this miracle girl. After a brief conversation she said it best.

"Girl, God gave you a second chance," she told Layla, "Don't waste it!"

Day 46: Wednesday, July 6th

Before we could roam the hospital, I had to be trained on seizures. I hadn't really thought about them because I didn't witness the only one she had, which was at the scene of the accident. Seizures were common after a brain injury, and most people end up on meds to prevent them. It was a precaution, as she would still be at risk for six months.

Now that we weren't confined to the second floor, there were so many places I wanted to show Layla, starting with the coffee shop. We had to take our field trips in between her therapies, and I was still required to take her in the wheelchair if we left the second floor. She'd fuss about it. She knew she could walk and didn't grasp the dangers of doing it without supervision. I had to constantly change her focus about it, and she was constantly telling me not to help her.

I took her for coffee at the shop on the second floor, then to the apothecary to buy shirts and snacks. While inside, a woman approached me. I was watching Layla pick out candy from a distance, thinking about how far she'd come. The woman said they had checked in a few weeks ago, and she'd noticed our frequents walks in the hall. Her person was still unconscious, but it gave her hope when her nurse told her Layla arrived unconscious, too. We were having a moment when Layla loudly interrupted from a distance and asked if I knew this woman. She wanted to know why I was talking to her. It made us laugh at the childlikeness of the interruption and the questions that came with it. I'm sure that lady needed a laugh. I was too familiar with the feeling of waiting for someone to wake up. I gave her a hug and told her where our room was just in case she needed to talk.

When we returned to the room, the case manager stopped by. Layla's discharge date was dependent on her progress. The faster she healed, the quicker our date approached. The original date was August 3rd, but Layla had bypassed a lot of milestones in a short amount of time. Shepherd was forced to move the date up to July 20th. She told me this apologetically, as if this would upset me, but it was quite the opposite. I was trained to care for her now and no longer scared of doing it outside these walls. Her news brought us two weeks closer to home. I called Jeremiah; it was time to book some airline tickets.

When you are admitted into Shepherd, you are assigned to a team. This way, you typically work with the same therapists and doctors and pretty much the same nurses. You must really trust these people to care about your loved one and your loved one to trust them. There must be some special kind of hiring requirements or something they put in the employee break lounge because they are such beautiful souls who love my daughter fiercely. They were with us in the beginning when she could only lay there and move her fingers and toes, and they've celebrated every milestone with us since. They've comforted us and informed us. They've shared their stories with us. Some have prayed with us. They make sure we are eating and resting. In the past 24 hours, several have even cried happy tears with us. She's moving at a speed that is not something you typically see. Several have told me how unusual this is, and it's exciting for them. One nurse told me, "I'm just really glad I got to witness this personally." Another told me, "There's just something really special happening to your girl." They are genuinely amazed. Most of them know it's God. Today I was told her discharge date has been moved up to July 20. There's been a lot of celebrating this afternoon. She is ready for the next chapter. We will move out of Shepherd and live in the housing here as she begins the outpatient program at Pathways July 21st. It's 5 days a week for 3-4 hours a day. Other than that, we

197

are free to do what we want. They say it can take 6-10 weeks to clear to go home, but this is Layla we are talking about. She has a big God behind her so we will see. We are comfortable here but ready for the next part of this journey and to be reunited with the rest of the family.

Day 47: Thursday, July 7th

One of the more interesting parts of a brain injury is the bluntness afterwards. Some will grow out of it, but not everyone. Patients will basically say what everyone is thinking but would never say out loud. I had read up on it, and doctors warned me. Of course, Layla was somewhat blunt before the accident, so I was bracing myself for a heavy dose of truth. She had already started doing it here and there. Usually it was harmless, but we were at Shepherd, so people were more forgiving here. We hadn't gone into the real world yet.

The tough part with brain injury? It's invisible. How was I going to explain why my daughter had no filter but looked like a normal girl? Other than her scars, you'd never believe she was even injured. She walked a little slower and her speech was impaired but not enough to recognize she had a disability.

Today, her occupational therapist, Emily, had an outing planned for Layla. They often take the patients on outings based on what their personality was like before. I knew from the beginning Layla was going to like Emily. She seemed to be tuned into this girl world with an appreciation of all the things Layla also liked. So, Emily decided to take Layla to get her nails done. There was one rule: No long nails. They didn't want it to interfere with therapy. I laughed inside wondering how they were going to stop her. I had taken Layla to get her nails done dozens of times. While I always got the same white color and kept mine short,

Layla got the brightest pinks and longest nails. I even warned Emily of that! We were going as a small group. It was two therapists with Layla and another girl, and I tagged along, too. I wanted to see her negotiations at work.

It started with the wheelchair. Layla did not want to travel with it. She had been making a fuss about it recently and felt she didn't need it. Emily agreed, but Layla would have to wear the gait belt and stay close. I followed their car down the road to a nail salon and parked. Layla didn't remember me getting a new car, even though she had driven it once, so she wanted to see it now. Emily gave her a little time to explore the vehicle before we had to go inside. When I asked Layla if she liked it, she replied, "I don't like black cars."

There's that bluntness.

The goal was to get the girls to handle the appointment with minimum interaction from us. The first step was telling the nail tech what they wanted. Layla stepped up to the counter and explained she wanted a powder dipped manicure with tips, of course in pink. The nail tech started conversation about choosing the color from the pallets provided when Layla loudly interrupted her.

"What language are you speaking!?" she asked suddenly.

She wasn't saying it to be mean; she was saying it because she had no filter. The girl had a thick accent, and Layla couldn't understand. I wanted to hide. This was exactly what I was dreading. Emily stepped in and helped guide Layla through it. I stood back to watch and learn. This was going to be my role eventually, and Emily was a great teacher.

The next issue was the tips on the nails. The therapist in charge tried explaining to Layla we could not get long nails, but it was pointless, Layla was not going to let it go. It was like watching someone haggle over a car price. The therapist would give Layla a little, and she would only come down slightly in length. She was not budging. Finally, they agreed on a shorter length, but Layla would still get the tips. Internally I was giggling. I had been in this exact scenario with Layla 100 times, and she always won. When Layla sat down with the tech and asked how long she wanted them, she even added a little length. She ended up walking out of the salon close to the length she originally wanted. Emily just looked at me and laughed.

Can't say I didn't warn her.

Day 48: Friday, July 8th

Little Miss Persistent got her wish today and was cleared to walk about the hospital without the wheelchair. During her therapies, we took a walk to the Chick-fil-a. I was also being trained on Layla's care outside of the hospital walls. It was only a few blocks away. We needed more practice getting her outside of the hospital setting where things were safe. So many things that were obstacles now—the distance, the heat, or the uneven sidewalks. These were all things we didn't have to think about before. I was on eggshells watching her now. Everything outside seemed like it was trying to hurt her, and my mind was racing as we walked along. I wondered how long it would feel like this. Would I ever be able to let her out of my sight again?

The last piece of Shepherd jewelry left on her was the stomach peg. This typically comes out at the end just in case the patients couldn't take medications by mouth. We were no longer using the peg to feed her. She was cleared to eat all her meals by mouth, enjoying all the options. She had to prove she would consistently take her medications by mouth before they would remove the peg. The night before was the first time they attempted it. Layla had a unique way of taking medications before her accident. She would swallow pills with no water. When they handed her the cup, she proceeded to eat the pills one by one without drinking from the water cup they handed her. It was a sight to see—another glimpse of the Layla I knew. The nurses had a good laugh over it. Sometimes it was hard to imagine anything was wrong. She looked so much like Layla; she just walked a little slower and forgot stuff at times.

We were counting down our days. We had just twelve more before we would be reunited with Jeremiah and Cali. I was figuring out a plan to see my son before we returned home. I wanted us all under one roof again so badly that I no longer cared what roof that was. Home was wherever we were.

Day 49: Saturday, July 9th

Sometimes I joked with Layla and told her she was faking it the whole time. She was progressing so fast that it was hard to imagine she was the same girl lying in the ICU lifeless just a few months ago. Being at Shepherd was an eye opener. Many days they would make an announcement over the intercom for a graduation in the gym. This meant one of the patients would be going home. I attended a few because I wanted a better grasp on what leaving would look like.

I was not prepared that Layla would be getting so many of her abilities back. I don't think Shepherd was prepared for that either. We had equipment rentals already lined up for our return home. They had us order a wheelchair and a few other things to assist her walking and showering. We also had a hospital bed on standby in case it was needed. It was starting to look like she may not need any of it—a possibility I never imagined.

In the earlier days of this, I would picture Layla learning to walk again, eventually walking out of the rehab. I even had background music to it in my mind. It was something I replayed often in my head to make myself feel better. I don't know if I actually thought it was possible; it was more like a dream state I would put myself in to quiet the bad thoughts. I used it as a distraction. Over time, I started receiving messages from people about similar experiences, only theirs appeared to be sent from God. Some of them I didn't even know that well. Some told me early on, some told me after she was okay. Some were believers, some not at all. None of them related to each other, but they all had very similar, very specific stories. All of them told me they'd never experienced hearing God so clearly speak to them before this. I think God sent His message across my circle of people or people that would reach me, and those messages were delivered as they were needed. It was perfectly orchestrated. There were too many similarities in their stories to be coincidences. I was out of it in the early days, but I remember after the second person told me, I was thinking, *Did you already tell me this? Or was it someone else?*

At first, I thought maybe it was just something people say to bring comfort. Then I started to hear it more and more from random people—the same story each time. I thought maybe God really was trying to reach me to give me peace and hope. I don't really know how it works. I've never experienced anything like it myself, but I will never forget those messages.

I never told you this before, but at the very beginning of this journey, I had a dream about Layla. It was so real. It was her welcome home party. She was amazing, talking and laughing. I believe I had a premonition of what her future was going to be. I told my sister I didn't know what it was, but my gut was saying everything was going to be okay from the very beginning. I've never experienced that before. I didn't want to tell you before because I didn't want to upset you.

So, I had one of the slots on your family's prayer chain that kept a prayer going for 24 hours, and to be honest with you, I was kinda stressed because I wasn't sure If I had ever prayed for 20 straight minutes before. I took a walk so I wouldn't be distracted, and I just prayed for your girl. Like really prayed for her for the whole time slot. When I got home, I told my husband how hard I was praying (and this was in the very beginning, so she had not been making her huge strides yet), and he said, "She's gonna walk out of there." He felt it when I was out praying. Crazy right?

I didn't tell you this before. Monday night, May 23rd, I was standing in my kitchen praying for Layla, and I felt I heard God's voice in my mind tell me He was going to heal her. That's why I was compelled to show up to the hospital that day to see you and pray over Layla. I told the pastor at my church what happened and that I never really heard God tell me anything, but I heard Him tell me that.

During the first couple days after Layla's accident, I had a gut feeling that I needed to go pray at church. I went to church on a Wednesday morning, and on my knees with a few pastors, I had never felt the Holy Spirit so strong. After I prayed... and cried, I felt so much peace that she was going to be okay

Day 50: Sunday, July 10th

Layla always loved music. We had dozens of these crazy videos we'd make in the car singing. It happened less and less as she got older and I became less cool to her. I knew one day she'd look back at our silly videos, and they would mean something to her again. Being a teenager is something everyone has to go through, and I'm sure we all look back on it with regrets. I didn't fault her for it. It wasn't as if we weren't close; we were very close. But the silly videos and adventures had stopped as she grew up. One thing had always remained though: I was a sounding board for her problems. I knew everything about her relationships and friendships. I knew the girl and the boy drama, and most of it was documented in texts, since that was her preferred method of communication. She had a lot of questions as things were becoming clearer, mostly about friendships. She seemed to be confused about who her friends were and were not at the time of the accident. I was able to fill the holes with our text thread and repeat the stories she shared with me. In a way, it felt like I could give her some of her memories back in her own words.

We started using music to get her voice back. She had to relearn how to push air through those vocal cords stronger. What better way than singing? Even though she struggled remembering friendships, she could remember every lyric to every song she loved. It was impressive. She could sit in bed for hours singing along to her favorite songs. She'd keep the whole hospital floor up at night with her karaoke. We even made a few of those silly videos and recreated the songs we used to sing. Music is just good for the soul.

We took a second trip to the coffee shop. Last time, she chose to order a Sprite because she didn't remember her love of coffee. This time I pressed her to order a coffee and pick what she thinks she would have liked. She chose a hazelnut latte on ice, and it was in fact a favorite of hers. I figured there was hope in that. Layla was still in there. We just had to wait a little longer for her to find her way out. In the meantime, I would help with the memories, and so would our friends.

Jeremiah: Did Nicole and Dan come by?

Me: Yes, I timed it perfectly, so we "bumped" into them at security. It was emotional for Nicole.

Jeremiah: Why?

Me: She said it meant so much to see us walking hand and hand toward them and Lay looked so good.

Jeremiah: Awe! Did she remember them? Did she speak?

Me: She mostly remembers people but isn't sure of the memories together and can't remember who her friends are still. A huge part of her memories is gone.

Jeremiah: Yea, I'm worried about kids being jerks.

Me: So far everyone has been nice. I read everything. Her speech is pretty bad, it gets worse when she's nervous. She needs more practice outside the hospital. I just don't want anyone to hurt her.

Jeremiah: She'll have it soon enough. Best we make it all family or very close friends for now.

Day 51: Monday, July 11th

Layla's progress opened a lot of opportunities in therapies. They started tailoring it to things she used to love, like cheerleading. One of the therapists was well versed in competitive cheerleading and worked on some routines with her. She was unable to tumble or stunt anymore, but the cheer music alone made her happy. They also worked on some of the movements Layla did as a flyer, only they did them on the ground with a therapist supporting her back so she didn't fall. When they brought Layla back to the room, she was excited to show me something. She ordered me to start videoing, which is something she frequently did with cheerleading stunts. The therapist counted off, and Layla kicked her left leg into a heel stretch with a huge smile plastered on her face. This had been her favorite cheerleading stunt as a flyer. I had tons of pictures at home of her doing this exact thing in the air.

A large box arrived in the mail from Florida that day, and Layla was impatiently waiting for me to open it. Getting mail was one of her favorite things. When I finally got it opened, I was confused. It looked like a large, heavy, bookbag. When I pulled it out, it all started to make sense. Layla had tried out and made the school varsity cheerleading team before the accident. She had no memory of it, but thanks to my hundreds of pictures, I could show her. The black bag had her school team logo on the front with Layla's name embroidered on it. This was the cheer bag we would have ordered for the new season to carry her uniforms and pom poms to games. I was already starting to cry. Inside the bag were several practice uniforms. These were the ones the team would be wearing for the upcoming season. Her coaches had that much faith she would one day return to them, and it meant the world to Layla. It meant the world to me, too.

Me: OK, we just got mail, and this made me cry. Her coaches sent her cheer bag and all the uniforms for the new school year. She was so happy and wanted to wear them immediately.

Jeremiah: Now I'm crying, thanks

Me: It was pretty emotional. She got so excited and got dressed faster than I could help her.

Day 52: Tuesday, July 12th

Layla was finally catching on that we had a great room in terms of a hospital room. The walls were plastered with cards and pictures people had sent. We had many pieces of artwork with Scripture. We had banners and posters. There was always music on, and the diffuser was always going. It just felt peaceful in this space that we made our own. Sometimes nurses who weren't even assigned to us would sneak in for a break. They would say we won "best room" because the room had good energy. I also kept a bucket of candy for them always stocked, so it was common they would drop by for some chocolate.

Still, we were ready to go. Jeremiah would be flying in on the 15th and staying with us until the 24th. The girls and I would remain in Georgia until she finished her time in outpatient. That was the current plan, but things were always changing so we tried to stay flexible.

The team from St. Mary's was still following Layla's story back home, and I made daily check ins with Kathleen. I knew once we got back, we'd have plenty of resources to help us navigate into our new world. Kathleen had become a friend now. I knew I was going to like her from the second she rescued me in the emergency room.

Kathleen: I was looking back at Layla's story yesterday and how amazing just five weeks ago she was starting to move her fingers.

Me: I was doing that last night. You called it! You said give her two months.

Kathleen: It's easy to see how strong your baby girl is. I never had a doubt she would be anything but perfect when she came out of this.

Me: I showed her the early videos today. I forgot how scary they are.

Kathleen: How does she react when she sees them? Does she have any memory of that time?

Me: She doesn't seem upset; just says she doesn't remember. I think she is having a hard time differentiating between real memories and things I told her.

Kathleen: Makes total sense.

Me: Just crazy.

Kathleen: She is a walking miracle, seriously!

Day 53: Wednesday, July 13th

Today's therapy was going to be a cooking class. There's a full kitchen in the gym that was also handicap accessible. I was really starting to notice how difficult things could be for someone confined to a wheelchair. I was developing a new respect for the ones who had to manage this daily. It was the sort of thing I never would have thought of until my daughter was the one in the wheelchair.

Today, Layla was making a breakfast sandwich she used to make daily before her accident. She used to make two of them the night before school, reserving one for her dad. They let her write out the list of groceries she would need, and she remembered the ingredients with only a few prompts. Then, it was her job to execute the recipe on her own. Almost immediately after she began, she started getting dizzy and had to sit. Her therapy team tested her blood pressure, and it was, in fact, low. They laid her down and gave her some time to recover as they lifted her feet up. It started to worry me, as it reminded me of the neurostorming. This was the second dizzy spell she had in two days. The therapists assured me it was quite normal after brain injury because the body takes time to relearn how to regulate blood pressure. Once she was feeling better, she returned to the kitchen and finished her breakfast sandwich masterpiece.

She remembered all the steps, and once again shared her food with the man down the hall.

Her last piece of Shepherd jewelry was coming out today, too! It was time to say goodbye to the stomach peg. I had grown attached to that little thing. It looked like a small button near her belly button. Thanks to Jeremiah's help, I knew how to feed her and quickly unhook everything when needed. I was proud of those skills. There were a few nights I had to troubleshoot problems with it, which was not something you'd expect from me. I almost wanted to ask to keep it for a memory. The peg removal is done bedside, just like the trach, and only took a few minutes. Just like that, it was as if it never existed. Before we knew it, she was patched up and ready.

Externally, all her pieces were put back together the way they were when this started.

Day 54: Thursday, July 14th

Early in the morning, our case worker came by with news. Our insurance company had just denied another week of inpatient care; and our therapy team agreed.

Layla was ready to leave.

I had never been so grateful for an insurance denial before. The best part was they needed us out that Saturday morning. The timing was perfect, as Jeremiah and Cali were arriving the next afternoon. The plan was for him to check into the family housing next door, and we would join him in the morning after discharge.

I had to get a few things lined up for his arrival. One of them was his room and parking pass. My car would be moved to the apartment side. I went to the security desk to get his room keys and the pass, and I brought Layla along. Sometimes I didn't realize she was paying attention because she remained so quiet, almost dazed. While the guard was getting all our details, he asked if I by chance knew my license plate number. I did not. Then, Layla's tiny voice interrupted with a mixture of letters and numbers, which we assumed she thought was my license plate. We stared at her in disbelief before the guard asked if she was right. I pulled up an old parking app on my phone, and as it turned out, she was correct. My plate number was stored correctly in her brain.

The brain is so fascinating.
Layla is so fascinating.

So today we got to go for a car ride! She immediately took over the radio and played the music too loud, so not much has changed. She does have some challenges with being out now, like dizzy spells, but we just went slow. Typically, I'm always going 150 MPH, rushing to get to my next stop. It was nice to take our time and just be in that moment. We ordered Italian for dinner, and it made my night to see her grab the bread and dunk it in the sauce like she used to. Before, she would literally eat a whole meal of that. She's lost almost 25 lbs since this started, but I'm curious where's she at now because I've been feeding her nonstop. She has a CT scan in the early morning to check a carotid artery they've been watching, but it's only routine and should be our last item to do before we leave.

Day 55: Friday, July 15th

They took Layla and I down for a scan around 10:00 am. Layla was pouting because she had to get an IV for this. They were doing a contrast scan with dye. I kept reminding her that we got to leave tomorrow, and this would be easy. It was the final step before our exit. She was more aware of my absence now and giving them a hard time about going in alone. The nurse offered to let me stay with her and dressed me in this funny-looking heavy vest. This made Layla smile, so I modeled it with a few spins for her. The whole thing didn't take very long. Before we knew it, we were heading back to the room so she could go to her last therapies and I could finish packing.

As I was taking down the last of the decorations, her doctor entered the room. He didn't look happy. He looked worried, which made me worried. This time, he definitely had bad news.

He started to explain the damage to the carotid artery had progressed. I instantly started thinking about her dizzy spells. Should that have been a sign? We were going to need a team of specialists to examine her and decide what the next move would be. He started talking about a stent surgery, and I started to spiral. Another surgery!

We would not be going home tomorrow after all.

I had forgotten what exactly was wrong with her carotid artery. I remembered something about it at St. Mary's on that first day, but I never heard any more about it until today. Or maybe I did; my memory was failing me at that point. I needed to text someone who remembered, and Amanda was that person.

Me: There's a small issue with Layla

Amanda: What?

Me: They took her for a follow-up scan on the carotid artery today. Well, it got worse. Enough to concern them to hold the discharge until we meet with specialists. She possibly will need another surgery. A stent? Then I had to break the news to Layla without looking concerned, but I am concerned! I don't want her to be put through another surgery.

Amanda: That's OK. We knew she had a dissected right carotid artery after the accident. They did not want to address it at the time (probably because they didn't think she was going to live), but she did! It will be OK. She is totally covered in prayer. God has brought you this far; He is not going to drop her now!!! It's going to be OK. Trust and have faith.

Me: This is why I love you. Did they tell us about this originally? I couldn't remember but the name sounded familiar.

Amanda: Yes, this is one of the injuries they explained the day of the accident in the trauma bay. However, the left one is more dangerous to mess with. So, it's a blessing it's the right. I know you don't want her to go through another surgery, but she is an athlete. She is going to be back to cheerleading, and she will need as much oxygen as possible.

I was grateful she remembered that. Day one was a total blur to me now. Today, I was feeling defeated. Layla sobbed for hours about it, and as much as I wanted to cry with her, I didn't. Layla grieved because she wanted to go home; I was grieving because I was worried. I kept telling her we were lucky they found it now. Maybe I was trying to convince myself. The news had spread, and one by one, our nurses and therapists arrived to comfort us. Everyone seemed as defeated as we were, but they still encouraged us and tried to cheer her up. One of the nurses even went and got Layla her favorite Starbucks drink. Our room decorations were all packed up and ready to go. Now, our cheerful room looked gloomy, which matched the way we felt.

Jeremiah would be arriving soon. The issue was he would get there after hours, which meant I wouldn't be able to bring Layla down to see him or Cali. It was like the cherry on top of a bad day. We would have to wait another day, but I really needed them today. I was venting to a nurse about everything when she slowly closed my door.

"You will get your girl down there tonight," she assured me.

I looked at her confused as I explained they wouldn't be arriving until well after the hospital closed.

"You will get your girl down there tonight," she assured me again, "and no one will be looking."

She was telling me to sneak out! I was a rule follower, and the idea scared me. But really, what was the worst they could do? So, I decided to go for it.

I felt like I was in some kind of spy movie. Instead of dressing for bed, we put on our regular clothes with sweatshirts. I even wore all black, which was standard for me, but Layla insisted on pink. Apparently, she had not seen how this works in the movies. Then we stayed awake waiting for Jeremiah's text, me praying that this whole thing would work out the whole time. The nurses didn't come in to give her the meds that made her fall asleep. They never did show up that night.

Jeremiah: Landing in 11 minutes.

Me: Geez, you fast.

Jeremiah: We had a good tail wind.

ME: OK Pilot Rogan.

Jeremiah: Dr. Pilot Rogan, RN

Me: Gotta get you those scrubs. See you soon!

It was time. Jeremiah and Cali were downstairs waiting behind the doors that led out to the parking garage. Layla and I crept down the halls out of the unit trying to be as quiet as possible. We passed several nurses on the way out. I braced myself each time, expecting to be directed back to our room, but no one said a word. I saw several of them smirk before turning their backs to us. To take the elevator down, a nurse had to hit a button. We reached the elevator before this hit me. I turned and looked desperately at the nurse at the desk. She smiled and nodded as the button lit up. I couldn't believe this was really working!

We still had ways to go. We would have to travel across the first floor and past two guard stations, one of which would need to unlock the door Jeremiah was behind. As we approached the first guard, he deliberately picked up the paper he was reading, blocking him from seeing us. We were so close. We reached the second guard, and now, I could see Cali through the window. I wasn't sure how this would play out. Would he let them in for a second? Could we step out? How long did we have? Abruptly, the guard stood from his post, and without making eye contact, he said, "I am going to leave this door open while I go sit over here."

We opened the doors. There stood Cali, tears running down her face wearing her pink "Layla Strong" t-shirt. Layla went immediately to her and wrapped her up in a hug as Cali fell apart in her arms. In between sobs, she cried out how much she missed her. You could see the months of pain she was being freed from as she clung to her big sister.

This moment was everything.

220

It was everything we prayed for.
Everything we worked so hard for.
Everything that gave us the strength to fight another day.

For those moments, I forgot about the scans. We were together, and I remembered how good that felt. It was like being recharged. We would not lose this battle. We had God with us in every step, and with Him we couldn't lose. If it took another week to sort out the artery, we could do it. We did not get this far to fall apart now.

Day 56: Saturday, July 16th

Our day started with Jeremiah dancing into our room with breakfast. He had a new pep in his step. I think we all did. Cali was not allowed inside Shepherd, so he left her in the housing and ran over to us for a quick visit. Layla and I were confined to the hospital until the team of specialists came by to review the discoveries from the scans. In a perfect world, they would give us good news, and we could leave on Monday. I wanted to take Layla out on her first day pass, but we were unable to leave without her being cleared by those doctors, so it was a waiting game. We were getting really good at having patience.

Finally, around 11:00, we were visited by a neurosurgeon. He performed a handful of tests on Layla and consulted with another doctor. I had hundreds of questions for this guy, and he answered each one with tenderness. In the end, they did not feel Layla needed a stent at this time. The plan was to start her on blood thinners and monitor the situation for the next six weeks. This was the news we were hoping for! We would still have the lingering concern of the carotid becoming an issue, but honestly, we were living permanently in a concerned state no matter what. What was one more thing? I received another training before we could get that day pass. We would now add stroke to the list of things we would watch for each day, too.

I signed Layla out for her day pass, and we waited downstairs for Jeremiah to pick us up. The plan was to have lunch and sneak Layla over into the housing. She was not technically allowed over there, but I was breaking all kinds of rules lately, so it seemed harmless. I found an Italian place nearby, and the four of us headed over. Throughout the meal, I could see Cali studying her sister. She was noticing the obvious changes in Layla. Even though she FaceTimed with her often, there was something different about seeing it in person. It was probably concerning to Cali. It was like a watered down, very tired version of Layla. She didn't have her usual, witty comebacks, and she didn't engage like she typically would. I knew it was bothering Cali, but she held her comments until later. She was just rolling with it; I think we all were.

Afterwards, we grabbed some ice cream at the store and snuck Layla into the housing. The four of us mostly laid around and talked. We discussed what the week ahead would look like. We decided we would get pedicures on Sunday with Jessica, then return to her house for a small family gathering. I was curious how the rest of the family was going to receive this new version of Layla.

We only had until 6:00 together that night, and time seemed like it moved too fast. Before we knew it, we had to walk back over to the hospital and return Layla to her room. Layla decided she needed a milkshake and nuggets of course, so she put in a request with Jeremiah. For a second time, I snuck Layla out of the hospital after hours. She picked up her food in the parking garage and got another round of hugs from Jeremiah and Cali. We were almost at the finish line—just two more sleeps. Technically, it was another starting line, but the chapter at Shepherd Center was finishing.

Cali: I texted Layla goodnight, but she didn't answer.

Me: She passed out at 9, we wore her out.

Cali: She was really tired.

Me: Yes, but it will get better.

Cali: How come she's not like her old self?

Me: Because it takes time, she is still healing.

Cali: OK

So, after our doctor paused the discharge yesterday, her scans had to be reviewed by several specialists: a neurologist, a neurological surgeon, and a vascular surgeon team. All agreed she won't be getting the stent at this time. They want to treat with meds for 6 weeks then do another scan, see how it looks at that point, and reassess. Reason for concern is she runs risk for stroke or TIA I think they called it. So, this gives God 6 weeks to heal that artery, plenty of time. Once they gave us the news, she got to leave the hospital on a day pass for a few hours, and our gang was back together. We even got to go to lunch, and we are all learning together how to help Layla. She tires easily but pushes through. Just seeing my girls together was magical, something I totally took for granted before. We got to FaceTime big brother at one point. She had a good day. We got back and ready for bed, and she decided she needed a milkshake and nuggets. Her personal food delivery drivers were happy to do it. Tomorrow brings a new adventure for us.

Day 57: Sunday, July 17th

We woke up and left as soon as we could get her out of there on a day pass. We headed straight to Jessica's. The plan was to leave Jeremiah and Mack back at the house while the girls went for pedicures. I knew it would be good for Jeremiah to be alone with Mack for a few hours. He needed to vent, and he didn't open up to a lot of people, but with Mack, he would. As silly as Mack could be, he could dial into his emotions just as easily. Jeremiah needed that kind of outlet, and I had always been grateful for Mack's ability to get him to communicate.

The nail salon was busy—very busy. This time around, Layla knew not to question the nail tech's accent. Instead, she looked at me for help. And just like Emily had done, I assisted Layla and explained the next steps. There we were, the four of us girls lounging in a nail salon having our pedicures done. The reality of it knocked the breath from me frequently. The whole ending to this journey kept doing that. It was the same feeling you get before you are about to cry, where your skin feels hot and the air feels compressed in your chest. I wanted to cry and smile at the same time, and the words "thank you" were on constant replay in my brain.

Later, we returned to Jessica's, and some family came by to say goodbye. We had been to Jessica's many times, but now there were a few new cousins to meet since the last time Layla had been here. She loved getting to meet them. I know everyone was feeling the same way we were. How is this possible? We couldn't believe we were here! Layla was in good spirits and seemed a little more like herself around them. Family is the best medicine, right?

That night, we would be saying goodbye to the two nurses we started with, Laura and Karen. They were the two ladies who received us on the first day and walked us through the first weekend here. They both worked Friday through Sunday each weekend. I had grown to love them. A few days prior, Laura had even dyed a piece of Layla's hair pink with her signature hair dye. She was sending her off with a piece of her. Karen was always dancing for Layla, and I would show her previous videos of Layla's many dances. She made Layla promise to come back so she could finally get that dance with her. It seemed fitting this was ending where it began: with them.

I had one more order of business to tend to: cancelling all that equipment that was ordered in the beginning. Nothing has ever felt so good. The lady on the phone made me repeat myself several times in order to be sure.

"We don't need any of it anymore," I said through tears. "My daughter is walking out of here tomorrow."

Day 58: Monday, July 18th

I woke up watching the sunrise peer through Layla's window. I woke Layla up so she could enjoy it, too; we even took a few pictures of it. Our last sunrise at Shepherd. We threw on matching shirts—the pink ones my cousins had made for us—and sat on the bed and waited. Layla left a note on the dry erase board for the nursing staff, thanking them for all they had done for her. Above Layla's note, was the note Jeremiah had left her when he first returned to Florida, *"You are the STRONGEST girl I know, stay positive, Love, Dad."* I was again hit with how full circle this had come—where we started, all the steps it took to get here, all the tears, all the sleepless nights, and how much better this had made us. Finally, her doctor arrived to say goodbye and wish us luck. We just had one more stop to make before walking out those doors.

Layla's graduation would be in the gym—the same graduation I had watched a few times for others. The nurses and staff gathered while Jen began her announcement. She announced Layla would be leaving and heading to Pathways for outpatient. Of course, she had one more trick before she left. Emily supported Layla while she kicked a heel stretch for the group. Everyone cheered, but I could only cry.

Jeremiah met us in the hall, and we began our trip downstairs. The closer we got to the exit doors, the more choked up I got. It was happening; she was going to walk out of the Shepherd Center. We reached the doors, and I could remember the first time I had walked

227

through them, so scared of the days ahead. I looked at that sign by the exit again.

"Through these doors, wonderful things will happen."

Wonderful didn't seem like the right word anymore. Amazing, magical, impossible, miracles will happen. Jeremiah and I grabbed Layla's hands. I had pictured this moment so many times in my mind, it was almost like I've been there before. Here it was, we were really going to walk out of Shepherd with Layla.

With tears in our eyes, we walked through the threshold of the doors hand in hand, together.

> *Today we walked out of this hospital while 56 other families are still in the midst of their battle. And a new person will take over that room and begin their fight. I'm asking everyone to pray for the remaining families and the ones who didn't get to walk out like Layla. Brain injury is cruel, especially to the caretakers. I look at her, and it's surreal. I just keep thanking God for sparing her. My aunt always told me our children are only borrowed, but I wasn't ready to give her back yet. We walked out today; we WALKED out of Shepherd with Layla. So here we are, the four of us having dinner and playing cards. Same as before, but different. We have been given new eyes. I am so grateful for this moment, so grateful for all the moments, so grateful for all the prayers, and so grateful for all the support and people who made this possible. Mostly, so grateful to God for carrying us through, You never fail me. We got our miracle.*

EPILOGUE

After completing an outpatient program in Georgia, we returned home just in time for Cali to start school on schedule. It's like Layla timed it perfectly. We were advised to wait until the end of the year to send Layla back to school. The goal was to let her continue her therapies at home for a while as she adjusted to her new brain. I guess we all needed to adjust to it as well.

Two weeks into the school year, I received a phone call from Layla's school. Against both mine and doctors' instructions, she had contacted them directly about coming back. She mostly wanted to return to the sidelines in time to cheer for the first game. As expected, she had her argument ready when I told her it was too soon.

"Let me try, Mom," she pleaded. "Let me live."

How do you argue with that?!

So, with every accommodation offered, Layla started school a few days later and was able to return to cheer in time for the first school football game.

Today, she's different from the girl we knew prior to May 22nd, but then again, so are we. We're all changed, but change isn't always a bad thing. There's a new light in her eyes that radiates to the world, and I don't have to remind her to smile anymore. She does have to work a little harder than before. There are new challenges and physical limitations. Sometimes I tease her and tell her she was superhuman before, but now, she is more like one of us.

She still has a lot of healing to do.
And as Layla heals, so does our family.
Just like the doctors told us in the beginning, we'll take it day by day.

ACKNOWLEDGMENTS

First, I want to thank my editor, Sara Shelton. You have a talent like no other, and you made this a reality for me. You truly have a gift, and I thank you for making this book possible and helping it sound like "a real book!"

Oren, thank you for stopping to help a stranger and allowing her to insert herself in your life still today. You are one Layla's superheroes, and you are stuck with us forever.

Thank you to the brave first responders who sign up for an impossibly difficult job, not only on Layla's call but all the calls they take. Thank you for choosing to work on her and giving us more time with our girl.

To the nurses, doctors, therapists, techs, and every role that is required in a hospital, you will forever have my utmost appreciation and admiration for the care you give strangers every day.

My BFF Jenna, I don't how to do life without you! Thank you for always knowing what I need (even when it's dogs), being my voice of reason, and being there at every turn. I love you even when you make me drink banana smoothies. Everyone needs, "a Jenna!"

Thank you, Kathleen, for the comfort, love, and guidance you so freely gave me from the moment I met you. I told you we were going to be best friends one day.

Thank you, Amanda, for your unwavering, contagious faith and belief that Layla was coming back, even if I thought you were crazy then. You will always be my Saundra.

Thank you, Corrie, for finding us, being my guide, and sharing all the brain injury wisdom and not going to easy on me or Layla. I still owe you that margarita.

To our Georgia Rogan family, Mary Jane, Kerry, Bethany, Jonathan, Jessica, Mack, Sarah and Eric, you have always supported us and loved us, and we are forever grateful for your presence in our lives. Thank you for opening your homes, helping with Cali, taking the drives to bring us comfort or food, and making a bad situation a lot easier. We love you dearly.

To my husband, Jeremiah, thank you for stepping up when we needed you the most, even if you are bossy. I think you missed your calling baby. I love you.

Most importantly, I want to thank God for never leaving my side, protecting my heart from breaking, and the protection every step along the way. You truly never fail me.

About the author

Ali Rogan is a wife, mother, and first-time author whose debut work follows her family's journey through one of the most challenging seasons of their lives. Married to Jeremiah, her husband of 19 years, and mother to three children, Ali's world was changed after an accident left her daughter, Layla, fighting for her life and recovering from a traumatic brain injury.

Inspired by their own story and the incredible first responders, healthcare workers, therapists, and fellow patients and families traversing the same road, she now dedicates much of her downtime to helping other families as they navigate the challenges of supporting and caring for loved ones with traumatic brain injuries. Before adding author to her list of accomplishments, Ali kicked off a career in mortgage lending in 2001 and has spent the last 20+ years helping people achieve their dreams of owning a home, something that is very personal to her. When she's not working, writing, or encouraging others, you can find her at the beach (her happy place), studying health and nutrition (her other passion), cooking for her friends and family (her stress reliever), or focusing on her faith (her lifeline in this world). An avid reader, and longtime lover of stories, Ali is proud to add her book to your personal shelves and share this story with the world.

You can follow Layla's journey on Instagram @ Laylas_TBI_Journey

Printed in Great Britain
by Amazon